The Beier Brewing Co., Boise, ID

To achieve immortality, astronomers discover comets, geniuses leave works of art, and rich people endow buildings. Peggy and Gerry Beier have conferred the honor upon Barney, a Newfoundland who died in 1993. They called him Barn Dog, and they named their Barn Dog Brown Ale after him. . . .

Bill Owens, Hayward, CA

In 1989, Bill Owens's accountant was going through a nasty, bitter divorce. Owens's idea of empathy was to brew a bitter ale, name it Alimony Ale, and design a label that, on one side, was a want ad for a new woman. . . .

Hair of the Dog Brewing Company, Inc., Portland, OR

To properly inaugurate their brewery, Doug Henderson and Alan Sprintz decided they needed a live dog to make its contribution. Since the man who was pouring the concrete floor just happened to have his dog along, the owners borrowed the canine and ceremoniously plopped its paws into the wet cement. . . .

Schirf Brewing Company, Park City, UT

Schirf Brewing Company is very nearly an oxymoron. It's in a state where about fifty percent of the population—the Mormons—don't drink. Says president and founder Gregory Schirf, "When fifty percent of the market doesn't consume our product, it's incumbent for *us* to drink it. . . ."

PREMIER

BEER

A GUIDE TO AMERICA'S BEST BOTTLED MICROBREWS

ELAINE LOUIE

POCKET BOOKS

New York   London   Toronto   Sydney   Tokyo   Singapore

An *Original* Publication of POCKET BOOKS

POCKET BOOKS, a division of Simon & Schuster Inc.
1230 Avenue of the Americas, New York, NY 10020

Louie, Elaine.
 Premier beer : a guide to America's best bottled microbrews / Elaine Louie.
  p. cm.
 Includes bibliographical references.
 ISBN 0-671-53676-1 (pbk.)
  1. Beer industry—United States. 2. Microbreweries—United States. 3. Brewing industry—United States. I. Title.
 HD9397.U52L68   1996
 663'.42'029673—dc20   96-21554
                                                        CIP

First Pocket Books trade paperback printing September 1996

10 9 8 7 6 5 4 3 2 1

POCKET and colophon are registered trademarks of Simon & Schuster Inc.

Cover design by Joe Perez
Cover photo by Beth Galton
Text design by Stanley S. Drate/Folio Graphics Co., Inc.

Printed in the U.S.A.

INTRODUCTION

There is a flavor revolution in America. People are discovering the joys of eating sweet corn, picked that same morning at dawn. They are sipping coffee made from freshly ground beans, scented with hazelnut, and brewed dark as pitch. And across the country, from Anchorage, Alaska, east to Brooklyn, New York, people are drinking beers like a freshly made stout with an aroma of chocolate and espresso, a beautifully balanced body, neither too sweet nor too bitter, whose flavor gently lingers, suggesting the possibility of having another.

Drinking beer is no longer just about quenching thirst, of chugging an anonymous bland pale liquid from an aluminum can. Because of the microbrewery movement, beers now possess as many flavors as there are styles of beers and brewmasters to make them. Throughout the United States, people can drink the beers of England, Germany, Belgium, and Ireland—without ever leaving home.

There are beers that are crisp and light, and those that are rich, heavy and winey. Some are flavored with herbs like coriander, a spice used hundreds of years ago. Others are made with pumpkin, nutmeg, and allspice. There are beers that lean toward the malty and slightly sweet, while others are distinctly bitter, full of hops. For those who like beer fruity, there are beers made with raspberries, strawberries, or marionberries. For those who like their beers to have the flavor of the grain, there are beers that hint of wheat or oatmeal. Just as beers are no longer interchangeable, neither are they the same color. Beers range from the palest gold to copper to amber to chocolate brown and, finally, black. Drinking beer is a liquid adventure in taste.

In 1994, there were 518 regional breweries, microbreweries, and brewpubs in the United States, producing delicate wheat beers smelling so slightly of lemon, hoppy India pale ales, and round-in-the-mouth, malty brown ales. There are lagers to be drunk while mowing the lawn, and thick imperial stouts, brewed to be drunk very slowly on bitter winter nights.

Of the country's microbreweries, only one in ten choose to bottle their wares. This book is a guide to more than eighty microbreweries, and more than four hundred different beers.

In the United States, the history of beer is as old as the country itself—the Pilgrims brought beer, and both George Washington and Samuel Adams were home brewers. At the turn of the century, there were almost two thousand breweries. Then came Prohibition from 1920 to 1933. In 1939, there were 605 breweries in the country; by 1974, only 39. The big companies like Anheuser-Busch and Miller took over the smaller breweries and eliminated the wide variety of flavors that Americans once drank. Gone were the Irish cream ales, Scotch ales, and wheat beers of old, replaced by blander brews—eviscerated lagers made to quench the thirst but not to delight the palate.

Then, the flavor revolution.

In 1965, Fritz Maytag bought Anchor Brewing Company in San Francisco, which had been in existence since 1851, revived the flagship beer—Anchor Steam Beer, with its rich, creamy, hoppy palate—and returned flavor to American beer. In 1976, Jack McAuliffe opened the first microbrewery in the United

States since Prohibition, New Albion in Sonoma, California. A movement was born.

Although only 10 to 12 percent of the microbreweries bottle their beers for commercial sale, it is those beers, lining the shelves of the supermarkets, that will reach the most Americans. "The big breweries have been playing the middle keys," said Bill Owens, publisher of *Beer, the Magazine* and *The American Brewer* and also the brewer of two famous American beers—Pumpkin Ale and Alimony Ale (the latter clearly hoppy). "Now we're playing the whole spectrum . . . the white beers, to blond and gold, to reds to browns and blacks."

The History of Beer

Beer, as drunk by the ancients, was not what we drink today: the gently alcoholic brew made of malted grain (usually barley), hops, yeast, and water. The malted barley imparts sweetness to the liquid; the hops lend aroma and bitterness; and yeast ferments the sugar into alcohol.

Five thousand years ago, the Egyptians, inventors of the first 365-day calendar, were also the first people known to have brewed beer made from barley. In medieval Belgium, monks made beer, and in England it was often the alewives who sold the beer at market and at their alehouses. People brewed for weddings, midsummer, and Christmas, and flavored the beers with juniper, coriander, and raspberries—as well as the leaves and bark of the ash and oak trees.

By the eleventh century, the Germans had discovered hops, a climbing vine whose pale green cone-shaped flowers perfume, bitter, and preserve the fragile, changeable liquid. Although the Germans had discovered what would come to be the classic recipe for beer, it wasn't until the nineteenth century that brewers chose hops over herbs and bark as the primary bittering and preserving agent.

In the American microbrewery movement, the brewery owners and brewmasters are a delightfully motley, generous group of mostly men (and a dozen or so women), who are united by their passion to brew, their willingness to share knowledge with fledgling brewers, and their happiness in being brewers.

There are several categories of brewery owners. The very youngest are in their twenties, young men who started brewing when they started drinking and haven't stopped. Then there are restaurateurs and wine mavens, anywhere in age from twenty-five to forty-five, who branched out into brewing as an expansion of the art of food. (Beer is a food, of sorts.) A few microbrewers are refugees from big breweries like Anheuser-Busch, who have rejected the world of Budweiser in favor of making small batches of infinitely tastier beer. And there is a final category: midlife-crisis brewers, men who were doctors, geologists, carpenters, salesmen, or teachers who either burned out, were fired, or prematurely retired. As they cast about for second careers, they discovered microbrewing, and it was nothing less than an epiphany.

How Beer Is Made

Beer production is a form of cooking, a splendid alchemy that results in a drink that can range from pale golden with citrus notes to dark and roasty with hints of bittersweet chocolate.

Traditionally, brewers steep barley in water until it germinates (grows a sprout of nearly an inch), and then dry it in a kiln. This is malted barley, which, depending on the duration and temperature of the kilning, can be pale and blond or pitch black. The lighter the color, the greater the sugar, and vice versa. The darker malts, kilned longer, produce the lovely colors for ambers, porters, and stouts, but the least amount of sugar. Malted barley can then be roasted. Or, the brewer may choose to roast unmalted barley. When brewed, the grain—whether malted, roasted, or left unmalted—offers flavors that can range from nuts to caramel to coffee. The flavors are allusive, not necessarily literal.

The malted barley is milled into small pieces, opening up the starch sac, which will convert first to sugar and later, via fermentation, into alcohol.

Then the brewing of beer begins. There are different methods of brewing, but the production of ales is the predominant technique in microbreweries, where adjuncts like rice and corn are not used.

The brewer puts the milled grains, an assortment of malts chosen for flavor, character, and color, into a mash tun (a stainless steel tank with a slotted floor), where hot water is repeatedly sprayed over it and drained, again and again. At 190°F, amylase, an enzyme in the core of the grain, converts the starch to sugar and turns the malt liquid into cloyingly sweet wort which, naturally, calls for bitter hops.

The brewer transfers the wort to a kettle and boils it for one to two hours, adding hops once, twice, or three times for bittering and for aroma. (The less added hops, the cheaper it is to make beer.) Like wine, a well-made beer possesses a nose, and it is this perfume, whether floral, fruity, or nutty, that hints at what the beer may taste like. An aroma is a prelude to the drinking. It invites or repels.

As the wort boils, some of the sugar caramelizes, darkening the mixture. When the boiling is done, the brewer (or his cellar rats) removes the wort, chills it, puts it into fermentation vessels, and pitches (tosses) yeast into it.

Ale yeasts are top-fermenting, lager yeasts are bottom-fermenting. Ales ferment five to eight days at 65° to 75°F and are then transferred to a storage tank, where some ferment yet again. Storage can also be for a second fermentation or to clarify, age, or smooth the flavors of a young beer. During storage, the brewer adds clarifying agents and carbon dioxide to carbonate the beer.

Lagers require two to three weeks of fermentation at 50° to 55°F.

An ale is a bitter, more full-bodied, fruity beer. Lagers are lighter, crisper, and more aromatic. But exceptions abound. Anchor Steam, a lager, is full-bodied and bitter.

Some beers, like wheat beers, are brewed to be quaffing beers, drunk on hot muggy days, so they are only 3 percent alcohol in volume. Other beers, like barley wines, are designed to be high in alcohol, 6 to 11 percent alcohol in volume.

Styles of Beers

Barley wine. An English term for a beer that is nearly as strong as wine. It is usually 6 to 11 percent alcohol by volume.
Berliner weisse. A white wheat beer made with malted barley and 40 to 50 percent unmalted wheat. It is a light, easy-to-drink style from northern Germany.
Bitter. An English-style ale with a pronounced hop character. It can be pale gold or amber, with ruby highlights.
Bock. The strongest (and often darkest) beer in a brewery's line. A bottom-fermenting beer.
Doppelbock. Double bock, an extra strong beer, sometimes 7.5 percent alcohol in volume.
Dry. A beer with reduced carbohydrates, low alcohol, and little flavor. Not to be confused with the German Diat beer, which has reduced carbohydrates but higher alcohol.
Export. In Germany, a bottom-fermenting beer that is not as sweet as a märzen, but heavier than a pilsner.
Hefe-weissen. A bottle-conditioned wheat beer, with yeast retained in the bottle to initiate a secondary fermentation, maintain and sometimes increase the carbonation, and enhance the complexity.
Imperial Russian Stout. A style intended for the czars, it is black, usually higher alcohol, and very rich.
India pale ale. This ale was brewed in Great Britain for soldiers in India. To preserve the beer, brewers increased the hop bitterness and the alcohol.
Märzen. A malty beer, originally brewed in Germany during the month of March.
Münchener. The beer of Munich. A dark lager that is very malty and almost sweet.
Pale ale. A well-hopped, fruity ale, copper or amber in color.
Pilsner. A golden, full-bodied but soft, dry lager with a good floral quality.
Porter. Lighter-bodied ale than stout, with less bitterness and a lactic quality.
Scotch ale. A very malty, strong, dark beer.

Stout. A dark, full-bodied ale, medium-hopped, with notes of chocolate and licorice.

Weissen. A wheat beer brewed with malted barley and 40 to 50 percent unmalted wheat. Citric, with a tell-tale sour nose, it is a quaffing beer, sometimes served with a wedge of lemon.

Wheat. See *weissen.*

Belgium has produced its own lexicon of beers, some of which are just being imitated in the United States.

Abbey. A beer licensed by an abbey, or a commercial beer inspired by a saint, church, or religious ruin.

Faro. The addition of candy sugar (rock candy) to a lambic, a style made popular in Brussels.

Framboise. A lambic fermented on a bed of raspberries.

Gueuze. A blend of old and young lambics.

Kriedk. A lambic fermented on a bed of cherries.

Lambic. A top-fermenting beer made from local wild yeasts.

Saison. A sharp, seasonal summer beer from the south of Belgium.

Trappist. Six Trappist monasteries—five in Belgium and one in the Netherlands—make this distinct style of beer, which is strong, bottle-conditioned, and fermented with wild yeasts.

White. A wheat beer, generally bottle-conditioned.

Evaluating the Beers

At each of the sixteen tastings, we searched for beers that were true to style and started first by inhaling the aroma that wafted from the glass (wineglasses encourage aromas, shallow glasses do not), gazing at the color, tasting the palate, and hoping for an aftertaste. We looked for the proper balance peculiar to each style: full-bodiedness in a stout, a pleasing lightness in a weissen, and so on. We expected maltiness with the brown ales, and hoppiness with India pale ales.

We sampled more than four hundred beers over sixteen tastings, sipping the wondrous and the awful under the tutelage of Cliff Batuello, the head brewer at Manhattan Brewing Company in New York City from 1984 to 1985. He led the tastings of the beers, judging whether each was true to style, from the aroma to the palate, balance, and finish. Was an India pale ale properly hoppy? Was the roasty porter lighter than the same brewery's equally roasty stout? And if the beer wasn't true to style, was it at least *tasty?* Cliff has deep knowledge, a discerning palate, and a light heart.

Then there were the curious, eager, articulate tasters: Eric Asimov, Walter F. Bottger, Caroline Cox, Michael F. Doyle, Ben Gold, Malachi McCormick, Jim Osborne, Michael Pierce, and Donald H. Shaw.

Each brought to the tasting his or her own preferences and idiosyncrasies, but from the first sip everyone agreed which were the best beers and which were the worst.

Good taste, even perfect taste, stands out.

PREMIER

BEER

Abita Brewing Company

PO BOX 762

ABITA SPRINGS, LOUISIANA 70420

PHONE: 504-893-3143

YEAR ESTABLISHED: 1986

CAPACITY: 28,000 BARRELS

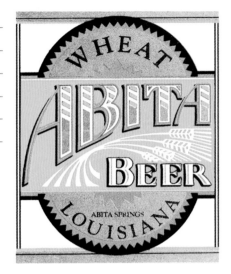

In 1986, Jim Patton, an instructor of anthropology at South-eastern Louisiana University in Hammond, and home brewer, had a midlife epiphany.

"Beer is more fun," he said.

"Brewers are so much more generous, warmer, and friend-lier than the academic world. Master brewers are happy to tell you what they do. In the academic world, you try to hide all your data."

So Abita was born, its beers designed for the southern palate. "People in the Deep South are allergic to hops," Mr. Patton said, "so our beers feature malt rather than hops." On a hop-malt scale, Sierra Nevada is unapologetically hoppy, he said, and Abita is the intensely malty opposite.

In the land of the crawfish boil, Mr. Patton wants people to drink a beer while they're cleaning that crawfish, boiling the crawfish, and eating the crawfish. "Beer is not a big deal," he said. "It's not to ooh and ahh over." Year-round he bottles four beers, one of which is a seasonal.

What he likes and the public likes are sometimes two different beers. His greatest challenge is the Golden. "The lighter the beer, the greatest chance you can have off flavors, burnt flavors, apple flavors," he said. "If you have a dark beer, the hoppiness and the malt will disguise the off flavors."

Abita Golden Beer is indeed light, so very light that it is almost inconsequential. As alluring as the Golden is to Mr. Patton, it is his slowest seller, while the Amber is the best-seller.

Abita Amber Beer is, as he intended, a sweet, malty beer. It has a neutral sweetness not unlike burnt sugar, the beer consultant said. It is a beer that may very well make southerners happy.

So, too, the **Abita Turbo Dog Beer.** Mr. Patton got the recipe from Peter Egleston, the owner of Northampton Brewery in Northampton, Massachusetts. In New England, the recipe was called "Old Brown Dog."

"We wanted to keep the dog motif, but while Old Brown Dog might be appealing in New England, around here old brown dogs smell bad," Mr. Patton said. One day, with the beer sitting in the kegs unnamed, the brewer was putting a basketball through a hoop and suddenly yelled, "Turbo Dog!"

The name is more intriguing than the beer. Brewed as a highly carbonated sweet beer, it has a very malty nose, a hint of caramel in the taste, and virtually no hop character. Someone called it puffy.

The most intriguing beer is the **Abita Wheat Beer.** The nose has a faint, slightly gamy aroma, typical of a wheat beer. Sip the beer and there is a hint of wineyness and wild honey. The aftertaste, however, vanishes.

For his seasonal beers, Mr. Patton, who is also the head brewer, indulges himself. At Christmas, he makes whatever amuses him, from bocks to ales to lagers. From January to June, he makes a black-amber bock that is high in alcohol and in malt. Summer is the season of wheat beer, and fall the time for an Oktoberfest.

RECOMMENDED: **Abita Wheat Beer**

Alaskan Brewing & Bottling Co.

5429 SHAUNE DR.

JUNEAU, ALASKA 99801

PHONE: 907-780-5866

FAX: 907-780-4514

YEAR ESTABLISHED: 1986

CAPACITY: 14,000 BARRELS

When Geoff and Marcy Larson moved to Juneau, Alaska, in 1980, they discovered that the state had frisky salmon, sunlight nearly twenty-four hours a day in the summer—and wretched beer. When the beer arrived at the end of the shipping line, it was sometimes a year old, four times its natural life. En route, the beer not only bounced around, it also suffered, because age does to beer exactly what it does to people.

Eventually, it kills.

"It was cloudy, skunky, cardboardy, papery," Ms. Larson said.

What then was Geoff, a chemical engineer and home brewer, to do?

In 1986, he opened the Alaskan Brewing & Bottling Co., the first microbrewery in Juneau since Prohibition. (Before

Prohibition, the city had forty-two breweries; afterwards, none.)

What the gold miners drank at the turn of the century is what the Larsons reinvented and bottle now: a Germal "alt"—which means *old*, as in a slow, cold fermentation—beer. Finding a list of ingredients on a 1907 shipping record, Ms. Larson handed it to her husband, who, in 1986, introduced **Alaskan Amber Beer,** and in 1988, **Alaskan Pale Ale.** Neither is pasteurized, and only one survived the two-day trip from Juneau to Manhattan intact. It was the Pale Ale, a beautifully balanced beer with a bright, light nose, a touch of malted in front that was sustained throughout—but that finished crisp, clean, and hoppy. It was refreshing and impeccable.

Less so the award-winning Amber. Beers are like people. What you see (or smell) is not what you always get. So, too, with the Amber. It started off with a toffee nose (good) but ended with a slightly fruity or what the beer experts call a banana finish (not so good). It was drinkable, though slightly flawed.

Maybe, as the beer consultant said, "it was a bacterial infection."

Maybe.

RECOMMENDED: Alaskan Pale Ale

Anchor Brewing Co.

1705 MARIPOSA ST.

SAN FRANCISCO, CALIFORNIA
    94107

PHONE: 415-863-8350

FAX: 415-552-7094

YEAR ESTABLISHED: 1851, BUT
    REVIVED BY FRITZ MAYTAG IN
    1965

CAPACITY: 100,000 BARRELS

When Fritz Maytag bought a bankrupt brewery in 1965 and began to brew traditional beers brilliantly and consistently, he became the godfather of the microbrewery movement in the United States. Like a godfather, he is used to being heard—and seldom rebuked.

"I am a man of strong opinions," he said.

He barely tolerates journalists who know less about beer than he. He will not send his beer to be reviewed unless he knows who is tasting it. He relishes, however, the humble, self-flagellating journalist who admits to being a mere acolyte at the altar of the godfather of microbreweries. Say "I know less than nothing," and he sits back in his chair and grins. "I like humility," he says.

"Most people don't like heavy, rich, strong beer—only a tiny, tiny, tiny percentage," he said.

So what do people want?

"Lawn-mower beers," he said. "If you mow the lawn, you don't want Guinness Stout. You'll want a dry, light beer."

He has beers for the lawn-mowing majority and beers for those who consider ales a rich, complex liquid food. The man may be prickly, as he admits. But the beers are not. They are delectable, friendly, and all-embracing.

Anchor Steam Beer has a clean aroma, a deft balance of malts and hops, and a taste that is rich, creamy, full—and engagingly bitter.

Sniff **Anchor Porter,** and there's honey, licorice, and caramel. The attack is sweet—the finish clean and dry.

The full-bodied **Anchor Wheat Beer** adds elegance to the act of lawn mowing.

At Christmas, are you tired of eggnog? Then consider **Anchor Merry Christmas Happy New Year Beer.** Each year, it's different, but last year, it was a bold, barley wine, the rich body spiced with cloves, and, after, a full-bodied residual sweetness.

Kvell over the beers, and the godfather will even admit he once made a spruce beer nobody liked. "We put in too much spruce," he said.

RECOMMENDED: Anchor Steam Beer
Anchor Porter
Anchor Wheat Beer
Anchor Merry Christmas Happy New Year Beer

Anderson Valley Brewing Company

14081 HIGHWAY 128

PO BOX 505

BOONVILLE, CALIFORNIA 95415

PHONE: 707-895-2337

FAX: 707-895-2353

YEAR ESTABLISHED: 1987

CAPACITY: 3,500 BARRELS

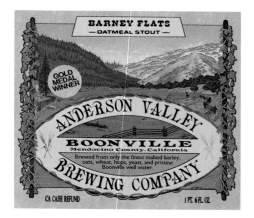

If Bill Owens, the loquacious, beer-happy publisher of *Beer, the Magazine,* ("I don't want lunch! I want BEER!") was exiled to an island and allowed only one kind of beer to last him the rest of his life, he would *not* take his own "Alimony Ale" (appropriately bitter) nor his "Pumpkin Ale." Instead, he would face death with the beers of Anderson Valley.

"The best," said Mr. Owens, who at the age of fifty-six has drunk tens of thousands of beers, owned (and sold) his own brewery, "Buffalo Bill," and through his magazine touts beer to more than forty-four thousand people.

What he and others love about Anderson Valley's beers are the deep, rich, extraordinary flavors. These are beers that do not need food accompaniment. Buffalo wings are superfluous. The beers can stand alone.

"Just like every brewery in the world, we use the finest of this and that, and all that stuff," said Ken Allen, owner, brewmaster—and a chiropractor. "But we just use more of it." Where he brews, in the town of Boonville, the people speak Boontling, a whimsical local dialect designed to be impenetrable to outsiders and invented around the turn of the century. In Boontling, a *forbes* is a fifty-cent piece (reshaped "four bits"), a medical doctor is a *shoveltooth* (the first doctor in Boonville had buckteeth), and Dr. Allen made up the synonym for chiropractor. "Dekinker," he said. "Take the kinks out."

Even in normal English, Dr. Allen does not speak like a beer technocrat. On **Belk's Extra Special Bitter Ale:** "We use gobs and gobs of grain, and come out with this special heavy malt flavor beer—and then we beat back all the malt sweetness with four different kinds of hops." The result? A full-bodied, full-throttled glorious maltiness, with a deep honey and molasses quality—and a nice, hoppy bite. Or, as Dr. Allen said, "Hoppiness may bring happiness."

In yet another moment of hyperbole, Dr. Allen calls his **Barney Flats Oatmeal Stout** "the thickest, richest beer made in America." He does not appear to be lying. The stout pours thick and treacly, has a very roasty, toffee nose, a smoky, chocolate, complex flavor, and a brief but memorable finish.

Deependers Dark Porter is full-bodied, with a roasted, lingering malt taste.

Where other brewers make gentle, almost too subtle wheat beers, Dr. Allen does not. His **High Rollers Wheat Beer** is honeyed, balanced, crisp, and clean.

Boont (the nickname for Boonville) **Amber Ale** is a tasty contradiction—both fruity and hoppy, with a dry finish, and **Poleeko Gold Pale Ale,** the last beer, has a touch of caramel and perfect balance.

RECOMMENDED: Belk's Extra Special Bitter Ale
Barney Flats Oatmeal Stout
High Rollers Wheat Beer
Deependers Dark Porter
Boont Amber Ale
Poleeko Gold Pale Ale

Appleton Brewing Co.

1004 S. OLDE ONEIDA ST.

APPLETON, WISCONSIN 54915

PHONE: 414-735-0507;
414-731-3322

FAX: 414-731-0800

YEAR ESTABLISHED: 1989

CAPACITY: 1,000 BARRELS

For twenty-one years, John Jungers had a double life. By day, he owned two Ziebart shops, which rustproof cars. At night, he made wine (the '70s) and brewed beer (the '80s).

He asked himself what was more fun—offering preventive medicine for cars or wooing luscious flavors, aromas, and colors from hops and malts?

The answer was Appleton Brewing Co.

Jungers brews lagers because in the Midwest, lager is synonymous with beer. But his passion is ales, which, he says, have more of everything: "More flavor, more taste, more fruitiness."

His **Adler Brau Marquette German Style Export Lager** is an example of truth in labeling. It is a well-made lager, true to form. It has a hoppy nose, well-balanced flavor, and a lively carbonation (lots of bubbles). It does what a lager is supposed to do on a hot summer day. It refreshes.

The **Adler Brau Dopple Bock** is mild mannered. It is roasty, toasty, and tasty, with a malty sweetness, but it is not as strong or robust as some aficionados might like. Drink. Enjoy. But hair does not suddenly sprout on one's chest.

The **Adler Brau Oatmeal Stout** has a deeply roasted aroma, a rich, coffee flavor with a hint of spice and cloves, and a clean, hoppy finish. It is delectable, although not as creamy as the name implies. (Add oatmeal to beer, and a creamy mouth feel is the result.) "It belies its name," the beer consultant said. He's quibbling.

Perhaps there are people who like beer that smells like Smith Brothers' Cherry Cough Drops, and are able to inhale such an aroma from eight inches away—and then completely forget the cherry in the drinking.

If so, **Adler Brau Cherry Creek,** a cherry-flavored lager, is for them. The fruit is in the smell; the beer itself is dry. It is a perplexing, contradictory beer whose allure is a gustatory mystery.

To go with the German-named beers, Jungers opened a Mexican restaurant: Dos Bandidos. But of course.

RECOMMENDED: Adler Brau Marquette German Style Export
Lager
Adler Brau Oatmeal Stout
Adler Brau Dopple Bock Beer

Arrowhead Brewing Company

1667 ORCHARD DR.

CHAMBERSBURG, PENNSYLVANIA
 17201

PHONE: 717-264-0101

YEAR ESTABLISHED: 1991

CAPACITY: 6,000 BARRELS

What does a man in his forties do when he is offered early retirement by a corporation—and loves to home brew?

He opens Arrowhead Brewing Company.

Francis Mead is one of the midlife-crisis brewers who are part of the microbrewery movement across the United States. (The other three major categories of brewers are people in their twenties, who have wanted to be brewers—not doctors, lawyers, or Indian chiefs—since they were eighteen; restaurant/bar/wine folk who branched into beer; and businesspeople who see money, and maybe a little love for beer, in the industry.)

Four years ago, Francis and his wife, Cynthia, bottled their first beer, **Red Feather Pale Ale,** and later, **Light Feather Golden Ale.**

Both are drinkable, neither exceptional. The Red Feather Pale Ale, an amber beer, has a faint, malty flavor with a dry, hoppy finish. It's a beer that you would be happy to find lurking in the refrigerator. Like its beer brethren elsewhere, the Light Feather Golden Ale is as its name implies light, in both flavor and body. The palate is minimal.

RECOMMENDED: **Red Feather Pale Ale**

Assets Brewing Co.

6910 MONTGOMERY N.E.

ALBUQUERQUE, NEW MEXICO
87109

PHONE: 505-889-6400

YEAR ESTABLISHED: 1993

CAPACITY: 700 BARRELS

Mark Matheson, winemaker-turned-brewer, switched from the world of grapes to the world of hops and malts for a simple reason. He was impatient.

"I wanted to be a head wine maker at a young age," he said, but it wasn't going to happen. After eight years in the Napa vineyards, he saw that his friends were still what the wine industry calls cellar rats. They rolled the barrels around. They worked for the prestige vineyards in the Alexander Valley and in the Napa Valley. But they weren't the wine makers. They didn't decide which grapes to pick, which wines to make, or how to fine-tune a chardonnay. In the world of beer, he could start as the head brewer. He could run amok with experimentation.

Now, at any given moment, he has at least eight beers on tap. The **Fruit That "Ales" You,** which (depending on his whim) could be flavored with blueberry, raspberry, or black cherry, is "the introduction beer." There are also **Kaktus Kolsch, Road Runner Ale,** an English bitter, **Albuquerque Pale Ale, SS Rio Grande Copper Ale, Pablo's Porter,** and **Sandia Stout.**

Since Assets doesn't bottle its beers, only one was hand-bottled for sampling: **Duke City Amber,** an American brown ale. Made with some chocolate and caramel malts, it has a sweet, roasty-malty flavor but is also highly hopped. It was Matheson's first dark beer. "It is," he said, "our best."

Just as he plays with southwestern names on his labels, so, too, does he improvise with recipes. Unbeknownst to the Italian pizza brigade, which has been traveling across the United States attempting to regulate an authentic Italian pizza (no smoked salmon, no goat cheese, no chicken), Assets serves an "outlaw" pizza. It is topped with grilled chicken and a red chili pesto.

RECOMMENDED: Duke City Amber

Beier Brewing Company

202 E. 37TH ST.

BOISE, IDAHO 83714

PHONE: 208-338-5133

YEAR ESTABLISHED: 1992

CAPACITY: 120 BARRELS

To achieve immortality (easy for gods to do, harder for humans), astronomers discover comets, geniuses leave works of art, and rich people sometimes endow buildings with their names deeply incised in marble. But there is a simpler, cheaper way to be known long after death, and that is to have a beer named after you, whether you are a human being or merely a very beloved dog or cat.

In Boise, Peggy and Gerry Beier have conferred immortality upon Barney, a Newfoundland who died in 1993 at the age of one. They called him Barn Dog and named their **Barn Dog Brown Ale** after him. If Barney drank English-style brown ales, he would not be displeased.

From the nose right on through the clean, short finish, the

ale, which was hand-bottled, is nicely balanced, with a soft mouth feel. The English would call it a mild bitter.

Tonia Schink was a family friend who died of cancer and, like the family dog, got a beer named after her: **Tonia Amber Ale.** Sent hand-bottled, it is a gentle, mild, well-made beer. Like nearly all hand-bottled beers, it is undoubtedly fuller in flavor at the source.

None of the Beiers' beers are overly hopped. "A hoppy beer is awfully bitter, and we don't like them," Mrs. Beier said. "If you drink a bitter beer, your taste buds are dead." She paused. "But that's my opinion."

RECOMMENDED: **Barn Dog Brown Ale**
Tonia Amber Ale

Big River Grille & Brewing Works

222 BROAD ST.

CHATTANOOGA, TENNESSEE 37455

PHONE: 615-267-2739

YEAR ESTABLISHED: 1993

CAPACITY: 1,400 BARRELS

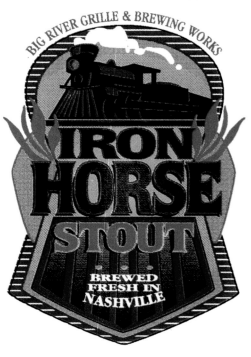

When people like a beer, they want to enjoy it not just at a brewpub but also at home. They want instant gratification. So when a brewery doesn't bottle, as Big River and others don't, what does a brewer do?

He has growlers, half-gallon jugs of clear or brown-tinted glass, which the bartender will fill with fresh, lively beer and sell on the premises. But with each growler comes a warning.

Drink within two days, or what was once delicious will turn sour and musty. Beer is advertised as the drink of stalwart, muscular, all-powerful men, but fresh beer is fragile, delicate, and evanescent.

Rob Gentry brews four beers year-round: **Trolleyman Wheat, Angler's Amber Ale, Imperial 375 Pale Ale,** and **Iron Horse Stout.** He also makes seasonal beers to celebrate the seasons, to celebrate a flavor.

Only one was tasted. The Iron Horse Stout arrived with a roasty nose, a hint of chocolate, and a dry finish. What it lost en route was an instant foamy, creamy head. But the essence was there.

RECOMMENDED: **Big River Iron Horse Stout**

Bird Creek Brewery

310 E. 76TH ST.

ANCHORAGE, ALASKA 99540

PHONE: 907-344-2473

YEAR ESTABLISHED: 1991

CAPACITY: 3,000 BARRELS

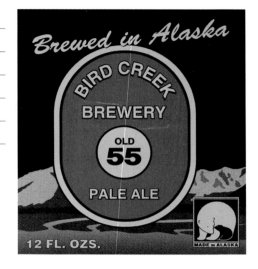

Ike Kelly, contractor-turned-owner of Bird Creek Brewery, recites the joys of brewing.

"Compared to construction, you're a real hero," he said. "The publicity isn't bad, the work is good, and the money is just starting to get there." In Alaska, even the weather is an asset. "In winter, there's a lot of darkness," he said, "and in the summer, there's a lot of sunlight." Both extremes—relentless gloom and equally relentless brilliance—make mind altering a pleasant, perhaps even essential, task.

He named his brewery for the tiny (population 100) town he was born in, and one of his beers, **Old 55 Pale Ale,** for the year he was born. The amber beer is not overly aggressive, but it is medium-bodied, with a slight citric tang and a nice, bitter aftertaste.

The **Denali Ale** is a weaker beer, malty but estery, and thin.

RECOMMENDED: Bird Creek Old 55 Pale Ale

Blind Pig Brewing Co.

42387 AVENIDA ALVARADO, 4108

TEMECULA, CALIFORNIA 92590

PHONE: 909-695-4646

FAX: 909-695-4648

The company is not named for a beloved pig that went blind. It is named for those moments in Prohibition when people went to speakeasies, sidled up to the bartender, and asked for a "blind pig." What they got was bootlegged liquor, stored in a mason jar. (Bottles weren't available.)

"Beer, wine, moonshine, it didn't matter," said Vinnie Cilurzo, the brewmaster and co-owner, with David Stovall, of the brewery. Not only does the Blind Pig possess assorted identities (speakeasy, legal bar, boxing ring, and brothel), so also does Mr. Cilurzo.

Between the ages of eight and twenty-two, he made wine at the family-owned Cilurzo Winery, also in Temecula.

"I helped crush the grapes, press the grapes, fill the tanks, the barrels, and the bottles," he said. Two years ago, he exchanged the glamour of wine making for the instant gratification of brewing.

"With wine, you have one chance a year, and styles you have to do," he said. "But in beer, if there are five hundred breweries out there, and 60 to 70 percent make pale ale, every one tastes different. Put the California cabernets together, and they all taste similar."

Although Blind Pig didn't start bottling until late 1995, Mr. Stovall hand-bottled three beers and sent them east, where two survived and one, sadly, faded.

The **Blind Pig Golden Ale** was spicy, hoppy, and full-bodied to some, and overly hopped, overly minty to others. Split decision. Your pick.

McNeill's Last Stout fared better than its namesake. John McNeill was Temecula's blacksmith who, on July 9, 1937, was the last man to be hanged in California before the gas chamber was legalized. He had murdered his wife.

The stout, a tasty testament to crime, has a wonderfully chocolate nose, but loses some of its maltiness in the taste.

RECOMMENDED: Blind Pig Golden Ale
McNeill's Last Stout

Bohannon Brewing Company

134 SECOND AVE. NORTH

NASHVILLE, TENNESSEE 37201

PHONE: 615-242-8223

YEAR ESTABLISHED: 1989

CAPACITY: 7,500 BARRELS

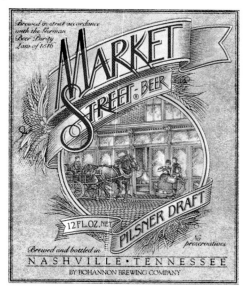

Mothers wean babies from their breasts, and microbreweries wean beer drinkers from Budweiser, Miller, and Coors. In both cases, the weaning must be done gently, or the result is trauma.

So when Lindsay Bohannon opened his brewery, he offered tasty but not knock-your-socks-off beers. "We're seven to eight years behind the Northwest," said Buster Williamson, a partner in the brewery. The owners didn't want to shock their customers' palates. They wanted only to entice.

First, they paid homage to the past by building their brewery on the same site as Greenbrier Distillery, which, in 1888, was the first brewery in Nashville. (It made bourbon.) For instant recognition, they named their beers "Market Street," which to a local evokes the street that has been home to companies like Jack Daniel's and Maxwell House Coffee.

Next, they devised a menu that was part generic pub food (Caesar salad, burgers, steak) and part southern (crawfish étouffée, fried green tomatoes, steak and biscuits).

Then they made beer. The **Market Street Pilsner Draft** smells like no other beer. It has the faintest aroma of potato chips. In fact, one taster even identified the brand of chips. "Wise," he said firmly. And no one disagreed. As odd as the nose is, the beer itself is delectable: light-bodied, clean, and dry. It is, someone said, the perfect accompaniment to French fries. A potato orgy for the nose and stomach.

The **Market Street Bock Beer** pours a deep, dark, cherry red. The nose is subtle, roasted, and alluring. While it looks, smells, and tastes like a porter, it is a thin beer. It lacks the full-bodied plumpness of a true porter.

What has gone untasted are their other beers: a **Golden Ale,** an **Oktoberfest,** a **Wheat Beer,** and a **Winter Lager.**

RECOMMENDED: Market Street Pilsner Draft
Market Street Bock Beer

Boston Beer Company

30 GERMANIA ST.
BOSTON, MASSACHUSETTS 02930
PHONE: 617-728-4182
YEAR ESTABLISHED: 1985
CAPACITY: 700,000 BARRELS

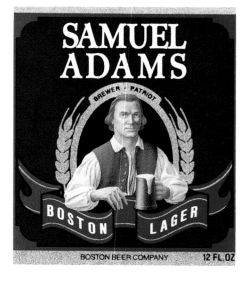

If brewing is a gene, James Koch (pronounced *cook*), the owner of Boston Beer Company, has it. He is the sixth-generation brewer in a family where all the men are given the first name of Charles, a middle name that starts with the letter *J,* and the family recipes for beer.

His great-great-great-grandfather, a brewer, immigrated to the United States from Germany in the 1840s, but generations later, when Mr. Koch started the Boston Beer Company in 1984, his father didn't encourage him.

"He said, 'That's the dumbest fucking thing I've ever heard,'" Mr. Koch recalled. But the father nonetheless passed the family recipes on to his son, helped to brew the beers, and today watches his grandson, Charlie, become the family's seventh-generation brewer.

The beer is named after Samuel Adams, patriot and brewer, and is one of the first microbrewed beers to arrive at American supermarkets, where it nestles by the high-end imports like Guinness, Harp, and Bass. ("If Koch had opened his brewery in Virginia, would he have called it Thomas Jefferson?" the beer consultant wondered.)

Boston Lightship Lager, at ninety-eight calories, is Jim Koch's retort to Bud Lite. It smells like a beer, has more body and malt than a Bud Lite, and is just bitter enough to pass as a microbrew.

Samuel Adams Boston Lager, the flagship beer, possesses the elusive quality of consistency. It tastes like it smells. The perfect balance of malts and hops (Hallertau and Tettnang) starts with the aggressive nose, carries through in the flavor, and continues on to the finish.

Like people, a beer can make a shy first impression. So it is with the **Samuel Adams Boston Ale,** which has a reticent nose but a distinctly tasty, malty flavor. It's not very bitter. But it is a safe beer.

Not so the **Samuel Adams Double Bock.** Traditionally bocks are the brewer's strongest beer, and here you can smell the alcohol. The nose is balanced, but the palate is intensely sweet and fruity. In the world of beer, sweet ones aren't necessarily bad. What they fail to do is quench the thirst.

The **Samuel Adams Cream Stout** is somewhat misnamed. It's not very creamy, but it is a stout, with a lovely roasty, chocolaty, coffee nose and flavor. Its cousin, **Samuel Adams Honey Porter,** has the lingering sweetness promised in its name, but isn't as fat as it could be.

RECOMMENDED: Samuel Adams Boston Lager
Samuel Adams Boston Ale
Boston Lightship Lager
Samuel Adams Cream Stout
Samuel Adams Double Bock
Boston Lightship Lager

Boulevard Brewing Co.

2501 SOUTHWEST BOULEVARD

KANSAS CITY, MISSOURI 64108

PHONE: 816-474-7095

YEAR ESTABLISHED: 1989

CAPACITY: 20,000 BARRELS

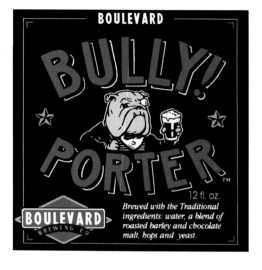

John McDonald, Boulevard's president and brewmaster, wants to keep his company local and sell (as he already does) more than 80 percent of his beer within a fifty-mile radius. His homegrown values are perhaps the reason why not all of his beers traveled blithely to Manhattan.

One, however, arrived in spectacular shape. It was the slightly misnamed **Boulevard Bully! Porter,** which is so chocolaty, roasty, and hoppy that it is closer to a milk stout than a porter. It is a terrific beer and deserves its exclamation point.

Boulevard Wheat Beer is a discreet beer, a quiet beer, a quaffing beer.

The flagship **Boulevard Pale Ale** is, as general manager Mary Harrison described it, "a middle-of-the-road pale ale." It smells as it should: clean and hoppy. Thrills it does not have.

Boulevard Tenpenny American Bitter arrived in a state of rigor mortis.

RECOMMENDED: Boulevard Bully! Porter
                      Boulevard Wheat Beer
                      Boulevard Pale Ale

Brewmasters' Pub, Ltd.

4017 80TH ST.

KENOSHA, WISCONSIN 53142

PHONE: 414-694-9050

YEAR ESTABLISHED: 1987

CAPACITY: 600 BARRELS

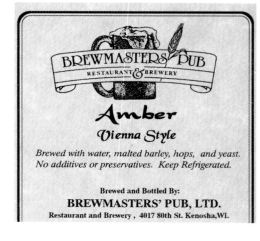

When Jerry Rezny started researching microbreweries, he met people who owned them, who worked in them, and who complained that the labor was hard. But he also met Bill ("I don't want lunch! I want BEER!") Owens, the brewer, writer, and beer-obsessor from Hayward, California.

Brewmasters' Pub is the result. Gone are Rezny's cleaning service and Christmas-tree farm. In their place are beers. The **Brewmasters' Amber Vienna Style** is a nicely balanced, primarily malty ale. It has a sweet, friendly nose, a taste of caramel. Because it is sweet, it's not the ideal summer quencher. Neither would it make a hophead happy. But it is a well-made beer.

Brewmasters' Kenosha Gold Lager Beer is slightly deceptive. The nose is pungent, flowery, hoppy, malty. Complex. But the beer itself goes somewhat thin and flat in the mouth.

RECOMMENDED: **Brewmasters' Amber Vienna Style**

BridgePort Brewing Co.

1313 N.W. MARSHALL ST.

PORTLAND, OREGON 97209

PHONE: 503-241-7179

FAX: 503-241-0625

YEAR ESTABLISHED: 1984

CAPACITY: 50,000 BARRELS

BLUE HERON
PALE ALE

Some people yearn to make wine. Others want to make beer. Nancy and Dick Ponzi do both. In 1970 they opened Ponzi Vineyards in Beverton, Oregon, and in 1984 they started BridgePort, which they bill today as the oldest microbrewery in Oregon.

But what separates a mature brewery from an immature one is consistency. New, tentative breweries usually have one delightful beer (the reason they got started), and two or three that are highly indeterminate, if not actually bad. By all accounts, BridgePort is a grown-up. Not only are its three bottled beers delectable, they are available to even the most penurious beer aficionado.

Housed in an 1895 former rope factory, the brewery allows its faintly impoverished patrons the simple freedom of nursing a half-pint ($1.65 to $1.90) from day to night. While the starving, beer-sipping poet sits in a corner, families nearby may be eating pizza, the parents savoring their beers, the children their Cokes. But no one is in a hurry. There are no waiters—only bartenders. Adult and child alike just belly up to the bar.

The **BridgePort Blue Heron Pale Ale** is what the beer consultant called a laid-back beer. You have to reach in for the malt, then discover the slight hop character, and then the chocolate. At the very end of drinking this well-balanced beer, there is a lingering, fresh aftertaste. Success. Subtlety has its own rewards.

So does lightness. The **BridgePort Coho Pacific Extra Pale Ale** has what many light-bodied beers lack: *flavor*. The ale has a pretty, dark golden color, lots of hoppiness, and a cohesive, balanced flavor. Its faint nose is forgiven.

BridgePort Pintail Extra Special Bitter has an aromatic, malty nose, but turns enticingly hoppy in the mouth. A nicely balanced, bright, creamy beer.

Not bottled are **BridgePort XX Stout, BridgePort Original Ale,** and the seasonals, each one named for one of the city's nine bridges.

RECOMMENDED: BridgePort Blue Heron Pale Ale
BridgePort Coho Pacific Extra Pale Ale
BridgePort Pintail Extra Special Bitter

Broadway Brewing L.L.C.

2441 BROADWAY

DENVER, COLORADO 80205

PHONE: 303-292-5027

FAX: 303-296-0164

YEAR ESTABLISHED: 1994

CAPACITY: 60,000 BARRELS

What happens when two ambitious little brewpubs—Flying Dog in Aspen and Wynkoop in Denver—couldn't make enough beer and were just about to leave their customers thirsty?

They pooled their resources and together built Broadway Brewing, a thirty-six-thousand-square-foot facility that has the capacity of filling three thousand bottles an hour. The brewery makes each brewpub's flagship beer—**Doggie Style Ale** from Flying Dog, and **Railyard Ale** from Wynkoop—and has made fantasies of expansion a beer-drenched reality.

On the theory that expansion, like charity, should begin at home, Broadway is planning to take its beers first to Coors Field, then across the country, slowly and carefully, state by selected state. Now Wyoming. Soon Illinois. Next, Pennsylvania. And after—New York, Oregon, the world?

Perhaps. Mike Magle, the general manager, wasn't saying.

The beers are brewpub generic. Doggie Style Ale is aptly named. It's friendly and nudges its way into your affections. It starts with a faint, malty nose, becomes more interesting, tasty, and balanced with each sip, and ends on a dry, hoppy note. It is good ballpark beer.

For those who like their beers gentle, there is Railyard Ale. Highly carbonated, its flavor is minimal, its aftertaste barely there. While it isn't memorable, neither does it offend. Someone called it shallow.

What's also brewing are seasonal beers including **Solstice Ale** for the winter and **Backyard Ale** for the spring.

RECOMMENDED: Flying Dog Brewpub Doggie Style Ale
Wynkoop Brewing Company Railyard Ale

The Brooklyn Brewery

118 NORTH 11TH ST.

BROOKLYN, NEW YORK 11211

PHONE: 718-486-7422

FAX: 718-486-7440

YEAR ESTABLISHED: 1987

Stephen Hindy, a partner in The Brooklyn Brewery, knows what ails microbreweries.

It's cousin Louie who makes home brew at home, he said.

What's drinkable at home isn't necessarily salable across a bar, never mind the United States.

Mr. Hindy, journalist-turned-brewer, has his beers contract-brewed at F.X. Matt Brewing Company in Utica, New York, distributes microbrewed beers from across the United States, and is a purveyor of the notion that beers, just like wines, have their own natural counterparts in food. He is a would-be matchmaker of foods and beers.

A few simple rules suffice. Rule 1: The more robust and flavorful the beer, the richer, spicier, or zestier the food. Rule 2: The lighter the beer, the more delicate the food. Rule 3: Or, as the beer consultant said, you can go for contrast. Drink a crisp pilsner with the most fiery food.

A porter marries with a beef stew, a stout with sausages, an India pale ale with curries. A wheat beer calls for salad and cheese, but a barley wine, slightly sweet and usually high in alcohol, goes solo as a *digestif*. Sometimes Mr. Hindy is very specific. "Amber beers go wonderfully with tomato sauce," he said. "There's a nice blending of the roasty flavors of an amber beer with the acidity of the tomatoes."

Brooklyn Lager is dry-hopped for a big bouquet, and is a dry, well-balanced beer with a citric undertone at the finish. It calls for salads, steaks, and oysters, Mr. Hindy said.

Brooklyn Brown Dark Ale has a roasted, toffee nose with a slight hint of hops, a creamy, balanced flavor—and a natural ally in spicy foods, whether Cajun or Thai.

Once a year, Brooklyn offers a black chocolate stout. Conventional wisdom pairs stout with a steak or a medallion of venison. But a tiny contingent is murmuring that stout, not coffee, goes with desserts.

One could quibble.

RECOMMENDED: Brooklyn Lager
Brooklyn Brown Dark Ale

Buffalo Bill's Brewery

BOX 510

HAYWARD, CALIFORNIA 94541

PHONE: 510-538-9500

FAX: 510-538-7644

YEAR ESTABLISHED: 1983

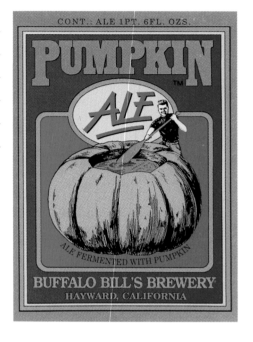

Some people dedicate their lives to finding a cure for cancer. Since 1983, Bill ("I don't want lunch! I want BEER!") Owens has devoted his life to beer.

He brews, writes, drinks, thinks, and, above all, *talks* beer. Beer, to him, is joyous, and he is its greatest proselytizer.

In the fall of 1983, Owens opened Buffalo Bill's in Hayward, California, then only the third brewpub in the United States. (The first was Yakima Brewing Co., which opened in January 1982 in Yakima, Washington, and the second was Mendocino Brewing Co., which opened in Hopland, California, in August 1983.) Although he sold the pub in 1993, Owens still brews and bottles two famous beers, which to the cognoscenti of the microbrewery world are household words: **Pumpkin Ale** and **Alimony Ale.** The first is famous for its recipe, the second for its name.

Pumpkin Ale, introduced in 1985, has been copied and reinvented from coast to coast. Some brewers use puréed pumpkin from the can, but not purists like Owens. Made with his home-grown three-hundred-pound pumpkins and spiced with cinnamon, nutmeg, and cloves, it is a delectable ale that contains the faintest memory of a pumpkin pie. There is a whiff of spiced pumpkin in the nose. The perfume is fresh, subtle, and light, while the ale itself is malty yet crisp. The ale is not cloying. It is Thanksgiving in liquid form.

In 1989, Owens's accountant was going through a nasty, bitter divorce. Owens's idea of empathy was to brew a bitter ale, name it Alimony Ale, and design a label that, on one side, was a want ad for a new woman. The beer was (and remains) a success: a hoppy, dark brown ale with a nice caramel roasted character. The ad was not so fruitful. The accountant is still single.

While some brewers immortalize the dead, Owens's beers celebrate the living. When one of his bartenders had a baby, Owens created **Diaper Pale Ale**.

When he's not having his beers brewed for him at Dubuque Brewing in Iowa, Owens publishes *Beer, the Magazine* for consumers and *American Brewer* for those interested in the business of beer. In the pages of his magazines, over the phone, and in person, he makes merry pronouncements on the future of microbreweries.

"Wine consumption is two and a half gallons per person a year! Beer is *twenty-four* gallons per person per year!"

"Now, if there are 525 breweries in the United States, they're growing at about three a week!"

"My latest count is 1,200 breweries in Germany, and we will surpass Germany in the next five years!"

"Ninety percent of beer sold is in cans!"

"For microbreweries, 12 to 15 percent are bottling—and bottling is the thing of the future!"

At fifty-six, Bill Owens calls himself "the only adult in the industry," but his enthusiasm is that of a highly verbal, wild child.

RECOMMENDED: Pumpkin Ale
Alimony Ale

Buffalo Brewing Co.

Abbott Square

1830 ABBOTT RD.

BUFFALO, NEW YORK 14218

PHONE: 716-828-0004

YEAR ESTABLISHED: 1990

CAPACITY: 7,200 BARRELS

TRADITIONAL GERMAN STYLED
12 fl. oz. **· BEER ·** 12 fl. oz.

Buffalo Brewpub

6861 MAIN ST.

WILLIAMSVILLE, NEW YORK 14221

PHONE: 716-632-0552

YEAR ESTABLISHED: 1986

CAPACITY: 600 BARRELS

Rochester Brewpub

800 JEFFERSON RD.

HENRIETTA, NEW YORK 14623

PHONE: 716-272-1550

YEAR ESTABLISHED: 1988

CAPACITY: 600 BARRELS

For Kevin Townsell, the owner of this mini empire of beer and food, his muse is German; his brewmaster, Fred Lang, is German; and except for **Limerick's Irish Red Ale,** his beers are German, adapted to the American palate.

Of the seven beers made, the public clamors first for the **Buffalo Lager** and then the **Buffalo Pils.** But the brewery's most seductive beer may be the **Blizzard Bock.** In the world of beers, a brewery's bock beer is its strongest, and at Buffalo, it lives up to its billing.

It smells like a bock—strong, malty, heavy—yet it isn't floral. Instead, it has a nice bitterness in the mouth, a subtle citric character, and fulfills the function of beer. It refreshes.

The Buffalo Lager is as light as the bock is strong. It has a highly malty nose, minimal flavor, and a lack of hop character. It underwhelms, but is Townsell's best-selling beer.

When Lang branched out into the ales of Ireland, he wanted to make a sweet, fruity beer. He has succeeded to the delight of some and the consternation of others. Although Limerick's Irish Red Ale is spicy and fruity, it has a slightly musty quality.

Lang also brews **Buffalo Weisse,** a wheat beer, **Oktoberfest Lager, Buffalo Lager Light** (ninety-eight calories), and **Buffalo Pils.**

As delicious and fulfilling as the world of microbreweries is, it is also fraught with occasional perils, because beer is a bubbling, living organism. Some brewers pasteurize their beers, which gives them a longer shelf life. Others, like Buffalo, do not.

Until 1994, Buffalo Brewing distributed its beers in twelve states. Then illness struck in the form of a yeast problem. "It exacerbated itself," Mr. Townsell said. "We lost a whole bunch of beer and had to bring it back from Florida and Chicago."

This year, as Mr. Townsell said, "We've pulled back." To pasteurize or not to pasteurize. To expand or not to expand. There lies the question.

RECOMMENDED: **Blizzard Bock**

Capitol City Brewing Co.

107 WEST COOK

SPRINGFIELD, ILLINOIS 62704

PHONE: 217-753-5725

YEAR ESTABLISHED: 1994

At a major-league baseball game, there are Budweiser, Miller and Coors. At the games of the minor league's Springfield Sultans, there are the Big Three—and Capitol City's **Sultan Suds.**

Capitol City Brewpub and Brewery may be starting small, but they're thinking big.

At the games, they start with four kegs, but are hoping soon to bottle, ship outside Springfield, head toward Chicago, and go on to Wisconsin. And if the Midwest should like its beer?

"We'll go regional," said Tom Goldstein, the brewer.

Meanwhile, he practices brewing a strictly midwestern beer—a medium-hopped beer. "That's the Midwest," Mr. Goldstein said. "We have a couple of people asking for something hoppier, and we don't have anything to give them."

On tap, there are a **Capitol City Pale Ale** ("just a regular pale

ale"); a malty **Capitol City Abe's Red Ale,** named after Abe Lincoln, with a touch of chocolate malt; and **Capitol City Winterfest,** a hybrid dark beer that is neither a porter nor a stout but something in between.

In a transparent bid to capture fans of Miller's and Bud Light, Mr. Goldstein brews **Lacey's Light Lager,** named for P. J. Lacey, a woman deejay on WQLZ. But what sells best is **Capitol City Honey Ale,** flavored with clover honey. And what purists would frown on is **Capitol City Australian Ale,** an amber beer brewed not from grain, as are the others, but from extract.

Of the hand-bottled beers, the Winterfest stood out. Closer to a porter than a stout, it had a seductive roasty, chocolate nose, a straightforward balanced taste with a nod to maltiness, and a slight sweetness on the finish. It is a nicely balanced beer that on tap is probably delicious.

RECOMMENDED: **Capitol City Winterfest**

Casco Bay Brewing Co.

57 INDUSTRIAL WAY

PORTLAND, MAINE 04103-1071

PHONE: 207-797-2020

YEAR ESTABLISHED: 1994

CAPACITY: 6,000 BARRELS

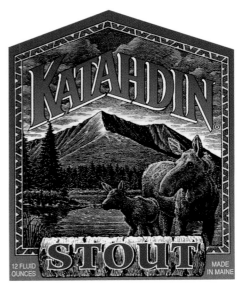

Michael LaCharite was the teacher of a home-brewing class. Robert Wade, a bored corporate executive whose specialty was supermarkets, was one of the students. They met. They talked. And Casco Bay, which brews Katahdin beers, was the result.

"I am a fourth-generation home brewer," said Mr. LaCharite, whose own sons, ages six and eight, may or may not inherit the same passion. He brews and bottles three beers, does not want a brewpub, but does want his beers, which are named for the largest mountain in Maine, sold in Vermont and New Hampshire. (*Katahdin* is the Indian word for "great mountain.")

Katahdin Stout is an oatmeal stout that the brewer said was sweet but the beer consultant said was dry.

What?

It has the classic stout nose, with the aroma of black malt, coffee, and chocolate. "It's like biting into a chocolate candy, and there's a little burst of caramel," someone said. And there's the proper lingering aftertaste. "More chocolate, and biting through it is coffee," the same enthusiast said. What is missing, however, is the oat flavor, but that is a quibble.

Katahdin Red Ale is an Irish-style ale. Specialty malts give the beer a lovely red hue, which asks to be held up to the light and admired simply for the color. The brewer calls the ale full-bodied. We call it medium-bodied, but it is nicely balanced.

The **Katahdin Golden** started with a pert, hoppy nose, then revealed a bit of fruitiness and a little malt. But the hoppy character, when swirled around in the mouth, went a little acrid. "It smells of a red beer," someone said, "but tastes like a light beer."

RECOMMENDED: Casco Bay Katahdin Stout
Casco Bay Katahdin Red Ale

Catamount Brewing Company

58 SOUTH MAIN ST.

WHITE RIVER JUNCTION, VERMONT
05001

PHONE: 802-296-2248

FAX: 802-296-2420

YEAR ESTABLISHED: 1986

CAPACITY: 20,000 BARRELS

What usually separates a fledgling microbrewery from a mature one is consistency.

A fledgling microbrewery may brew three beers, but often only one is palatable. The rest may be unbalanced (too much malt, no hops, or vice versa) or tasteless. Sometimes there is a taste, but it is odd: thin, sour, acrid, musty. But when a microbrewery is mature, all the beers are drinkable, whether it is a delicate pale wheat beer or a full-throttle gutsy stout. Sometimes the beers are delicious.

Catamount, with the eastern cougar on its label (once called *catamounts,* from the Old World "cat-of-the-mountain"), is a mature microbrewery.

Catamount Gold is exactly what the brewery wanted it to be: a lightly malty, slightly floral training-wheel beer. It drinks clean, but the flavor doesn't overwhelm. Eyebrows don't rise.

It was one of Catamount's first two beers, along with **Catamount Amber.** "Intuition told us that Gold would be the most popular because it looked American and because we couldn't count on a rapid change in taste," said Jeff Close, one of the brewers.

Intuition was correct.

The Amber progresses more deeply into flavor, beginning with the nose, which has a hint of orange peel, and segueing into a medium-bodied, balanced ale. What it's not is a powerful beer.

Catamount Bock, a seasonal beer, has sweet butterscotch, caramel flavors but ends on a spicy, hoppy note. "Is this an ale that Catamount thinks is a lager?" asked the beer consultant.

The **Catamount Porter,** however, has no identity qualms. It is an addictive, chocolaty porter, with undertones of licorice and caramel. Perfectly balanced, it is a smooth beer that finishes with a dry, hoppy flourish. "Some porters are cloying," someone said. "This one is not."

To amuse themselves, the brewers make seasonal beers, including **Catamount American Wheat, Catamount Octoberfest,** a Viennese-style lager, and **Catamount Christmas Ale,** a deep red India pale ale.

Within the microbrewery movement, some of the cognoscenti, like Catamount, are matchmaking beers with foods. Mr. Close likes to see the Gold accompany seafood—either tossed into the batter or drunk copiously with steamed mussels. The Amber, he said, marries well with pork chops and sausages, and the porter with oysters (the traditional dish), or, if served at room temperature, with a wedge of cheddar cheese and fresh walnuts.

RECOMMENDED: Catamount Amber
Catamount Porter
Catamount Gold

Celis Brewery Inc.

2431 FORBES DR.

AUSTIN, TEXAS 78754

PHONE: 512-835-0884

YEAR ESTABLISHED: 1992

CAPACITY: 45,000 BARRELS

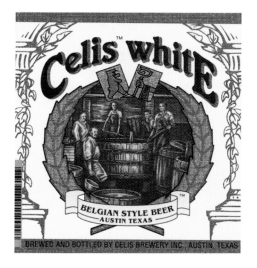

Wheat beer, or white beer, may be new to Americans but not to Belgians. By the 1800s, in the town of Hoegaarden, there were thirty breweries making white beer, which in Belgium is not as bland as it sounds. As made by Celis, it is *not* the white bread of beer. Flavored with coriander and orange peel, it is a gentle beer that, on afterthought, is spicy, memorable, and quietly resonant.

The story of how this newly trendy beer came to be brewed from coast to coast is the story of Pierre Celis, the Belgian founder of the brewery.

The American culinary world has its superstars—James Beard, Julia Child, Alice Waters. And the world of American microbreweries, not even twenty years old, already has its own legends. Just as Fritz Maytag is the godfather of the microbrewery movement in the United States, and Bill Owens is the man who brewed Pumpkin Ale, Pierre Celis will be known, perhaps forever, as the father of wheat beer in America.

In 1966, Celis was unhappy. Wheat beer was all but extinct in Europe. That year he revived white beer, and in 1992, moved from Belgium to Austin where the beer, along with some other styles, is now being brewed.

"There are two different Celis whites," said Peter Camps, executive vice president in charge of production and the brewmaster. There are **Celis White,** subtitled **Belgian Style Beer,** the precursor of all American wheat beers, and **Celis White,** subtitled **Hill Country Beer.**

Do not confuse the two. The Belgian Style Beer is, to Americans, an original, wonderful beer. It is flowery, honeyed, spicy, fruity—and even, someone said, gamy. Like it or not, it is memorable. It is so tasty (remember the coriander and the orange peel) that it can accompany sausage of venison or wild boar. Face-to-face with Mexican food, it will not cower in the background. "To be very honest," Mr. Camps said, "I have it with barbecue."

The Celis White Hill Country Beer is the lesser, unfortunate sibling. It has a bizarre sweet-and-sour taste.

Just as wine makers have a *grand cru,* the best they have to offer, so does Celis. "In the old days, in the small Belgian villages where there were three thousand people and thirty breweries, all those brewers used to make a special beer, or an ale, only for special occasions," Mr. Camp said. "If the daughter of the mayor was having a wedding, the brewer would make something special. When all the legendary figureheads from the town—the constable, the sheriff, the priest—would be together, the brewer would pull out the best beer."

The **Celis Ale Grand Cru** is a strong beer (7 percent alcohol), with a fruity aroma that has a whiff of summer blossoms and a full, malty, yet spicy character with a touch of butterscotch. It is to be sipped slowly. It is not a quaffing beer.

RECOMMENDED: Celis White Belgian Style Ale
Celis Ale Grand Cru

Champion Brewing Company

1442 LARIMER SQUARE

DENVER, COLORADO 80202

PHONE: 303-534-5444

FAX: 303-534-5490

YEAR ESTABLISHED: 1991

Michael Fahy, brewmaster and partner, left a career with the Big Three for the smaller world of microbreweries. He has no regrets.

At Coors, where he was a senior research chemist from 1976 to 1982, he helped develop Coors Light and George Killian Red Ale. Then he and the brewery had a tiff—and Champion was born.

"It's very easy to make a very potent, highly flavored beer that tastes like hell," he said. "It's difficult to make a light beer that doesn't have any off flavors and that is clean and well-crafted."

Fahy's specialty, then, is light beers with an iota more flavor than the Big Three: Budweiser, Coors, and Miller.

Even the **Home Run Ale,** whose nose is a cross between a

stout and a porter, is light. In the aroma, there is a smoky character and a little chocolate. The flavor is subtly sweet. Although it lacks the robustness of a stout or a porter, it has its own charms. It's a year-round drink, to be swallowed on even the doggiest days of summer.

Norm Clarke's Sports Ale, brewed for a local sportswriter, is a no-nose beer. Stick your own nose deep into the beer, inhale with all your might and then maybe, if your sinuses are clear, you will detect the faintest floral scent. It is a generic microbrewed, well-balanced quaffing beer, with barely any maltiness. Mr. Fahy describes it as a light-bodied pale ale.

Its polar opposite is **Larimer Red Ale,** where the malt prevails and the hops are barely present. What's left is a decent beer that some call "safe."

For the calorie conscious, there is **Red Light Beer,** where the emphasis is on the word *light*. The shade of amber is light. The body is light. The flavor is light, verging toward tasteless. Yet, on a miserable muggy day, it would quench the thirst.

The nose of the **Buckwheat Beer** is reminiscent of a lime rickey—citric, cool, sprightly. So, too, the flavor.

RECOMMENDED: **Champion Home Run Ale**
Champion Norm Clarke's Sports Ale

Cold Spring Brewing Company

219 NORTH RED RIVER AVE.

COLD SPRING, MINNESOTA 56320

PHONE: 612-685-8686

YEAR ESTABLISHED: 1874

CAPACITY: 300,000 BARRELS, OF WHICH 17,000 IS DEVOTED TO MICROBREWED BEERS

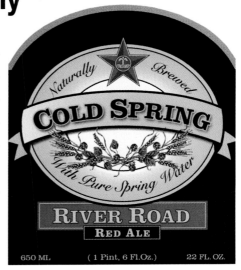

Just as Anheuser-Busch stared at the microbrewery movement, decided it was both fetching and provocative, and bought an interest in Red Hook, so, too, Cold Spring, a regional brewery, has started thinking small (as a way of thinking big) and turned its hand to microbrewing.

In 1994, the brewery, whose capacity is 300,000 barrels, brewed 17,000 barrels of just two beers: **Cold Spring Pale Ale** and **Cold Spring Export Lager.** Using the expertise from more than a century of brewing, Cold Spring has tested the alcoholic waters—and *likes* them.

The Cold Spring Pale Ale has the proper malty/hoppy balance, both in the aroma and the palate, and a clean, crisp finish.

The **Cold Spring River Road Red Ale** smelled of the grain and had a mild-mannered hoppiness.

With just 17,000 barrels under its belt, Cold Spring plans to go national, and is working out a licensing agreement with a company in California, said James Stegura, president of the company. (Since 1944, the company has been owned by Myron Johnson, who died in 1993, and his family.) Cold Spring makes the kinds of beers that could conceivably go coast to coast, offending no one, and pleasing most everybody.

RECOMMENDED: **Cold Spring Pale Ale**
Cold Spring River Road Red Ale

Dallas County Brewing Co. Inc./Old Depot Pub

301 SOUTH TENTH ST.

PO BOX 155

ADEL, IOWA 50003

PHONE: 515-993-5064

YEAR ESTABLISHED: 1992

CAPACITY: 8,000 BARRELS

No, the brewery is not in Texas. It is in Adel, Iowa, twenty miles west of Des Moines, in a 1907 building that originally housed the Ideal Sunbonnet & Corn Husking Glove Factory. Next door is the brewpub, ensconced in what was once the 1906 freight and passenger depot for the Chicago, Milwaukee & St. Paul Railroad. Both buildings are now devoted to quenching parched throats and feeding rumbling stomachs.

The food ranges from the mundane (Cornish hen, baked salmon) to the exotic. For the carnivore, there is a panoply of wild game. If he wants steaks, he can be undaring and have beef, or he can choose from buffalo, caribou, or venison. If he craves creatures on the wing, he can choose grilled quail or pheasant. If he likes his meat in tiny medallions, breaded, fried, and disguised beyond recognition, he can have turtle or alligator tail. (The latter is served with a cocktail sauce on the side.) Even ravioli, simple little stuffed pockets of dough, are esoteric. They are filled with rattlesnake meat and Swiss cheese. Turkey, of course, is wild, and the breast is smoked and served with a morel sauce.

The same midwestern palate that thinks nothing of tucking into buffalo steak is more provincial when it comes to beer. "Basically, Iowa runs behind the rest of the nation in trends," said Mark Hanley, the brand manager, "and we're trying to educate the people in Iowa to drink better, not more."

What scares the midwesterner most?

"Porters," Mr. Hanley said. "They have the idea that dark beers are bitter, and maybe a stout is, but a porter is a lot smoother." When he sees a woman drinking a porter, he knows a barricade has fallen. Since dark beers are the most foreign to Iowans, it follows that the lager is the most popular beer.

The beer is not pasteurized, but neither are they wild. **Old Depot Lager Beer** is beautifully balanced, with a nice malty nose and a clean, well-balanced flavor. It is easy to drink, and merry on the palate.

Old Depot Ale, an American pale ale, is malty, foamy, and almost turbulent when poured. What it lacks is a sense of hops.

Less successful were the year-round **Old Depot Porter** and the seasonal **Old Depot May Bock Beer.** Both went sour.

The brewery also produces **Old Depot Light Beer,** which has eighty-five calories, **Old Depot Oktoberfest,** and **Old Depot Holiday Ale,** a nut brown ale.

RECOMMENDED: Old Depot Lager Beer

Deschutes Brewery & Public House

1044 N. W. BOND ST.

BEND, OREGON 97701

PHONE: 503-382-9242

Deschutes Brewery Production Facility

901 S. W. SIMPSON AVE.

BEND, OREGON 97702

PHONE: 503-385-8606

YEAR ESTABLISHED: 1988

CAPACITY: 20,000 BARRELS

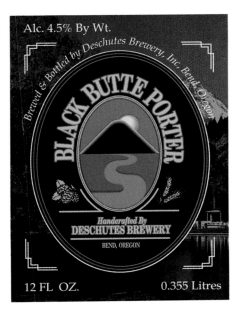

I'm president, but 'owner' I'm not comfortable with—the bank really owns it," said Gary Fish in a tone best described as Pacific Northwest laid-back. It is a self-deprecating, aw-shucks style that matches the equally understated Pacific Northwest manner of dressing: down jacket and jeans. (But one of the first lessons of survival in the Pacific Northwest is never to judge a man's worth by his drab, anonymous clothing.) For the moment, Mr. Fish is self-effacing. There's a pause.

Then, "Hell, let's get right down to it," he said. "I have two breweries and a brewpub."

Best of all, he has a terrific microbrewery (named for the Deschutes River) where the three year-round bottled beers are excellent, true to their styles—and addictive.

Proof that Oregon is part of the heartland of the microbrewery movement lies in which Deschutes beer sells best. It is the **Black Butte Porter.** Unlike beer drinkers in the South or Midwest, the people of the Pacific Northwest do not fear a strong and/or dark beer.

It has a bright, fresh, toasty character, with a full body and a nice chewiness. It is a beautifully balanced, dry porter. It's *food.*

Deschutes calls its **Cascade Golden Ale** its "transition" beer for those switching from American industrial beers to hand-crafted ales. With this beer, the transition should be both painless and inevitable. It is a delectable, tasty, and refreshing beer with an aromatic nose, slightly floral and hoppy. The taste is balanced, full, and rounded, with a predominance of the Cascade hops. The final reward is that it has a lingering, malty/hoppy aftertaste. Mr. Fish calls it "snappy." It is.

The amber-colored **Bachelor Bitter** is an addictive, all-purpose beer. It can be drunk every day, simply sipped on its own or accompanying a quesadilla, a plate of Szechuan bean curd, or a garlic-and-fennel sausage. Named for Mount Bachelor, which is twenty miles away from Bend, it has a luscious, full malt body, a chewiness in the mouth, and a classic bitter hop finish.

Since part of the joy of brewing is to make seasonals, Deschutes offers an **Obsidian Stout,** a **Mirror Pond Pale Ale,** and a **Jubelale.**

RECOMMENDED: Black Butte Porter
Cascade Golden Ale
Bachelor Bitter

Dock Street Brewing Co.

BREWERY AND RESTAURANT

TWO LOGAN SQUARE

PHILADELPHIA, PENNSYLVANIA
19103

PHONE: 215-496-0413

YEAR ESTABLISHED: 1990

CAPACITY: 25,000 BARRELS AT F.X.
MATT IN UTICA, NEW YORK,
AND 3,000 BARRELS IN
PHILADELPHIA

BOHEMIAN PILSNER

When I'm not drinking beer, then I'm drinking champagne," said Rosemary Certl, one of the owners of the Dock Street Brewing Co. For her, there is no middle ground.

Dock Street's beers, however, very much occupy a center space in the world of microbreweries. They are neither splendid nor boring. They are in between.

In 1986, Dock Street started having its beers bottled by F.X. Matt in Utica, New York, and in 1990 opened its own brewery and restaurant in Philadelphia. At either place, the recipes are the same.

The **Dock Street Bohemian Pilsner Beer** has a faint aroma

that could use a more floral character and, the beer consultant said, "more meat behind it." It is, however, drinkable.

So, too, the **Dock Street Amber Beer,** which has a fresh, clean, malty, and slightly floral quality. What it lacks is an aftertaste. It flattens out in the mouth with a short, abrupt finish. (In beer, an aftertaste is to be sought after.)

Dock Street also offers a **Dortmunder,** an **Old Ale, Pale Ale, Red Ale, Dubbel, Halles,** and **Weiss Beer.**

RECOMMENDED: **Dock Street Bohemian Pilsner Beer**
Dock Street Amber Beer

Dubuque Brewing and Bottling Company

EAST FOURTH ST. EXTENSION

DUBUQUE, IOWA 52001

PHONE: 319-583-2042

FAX: 319-583-0009

YEAR ESTABLISHED: 1991

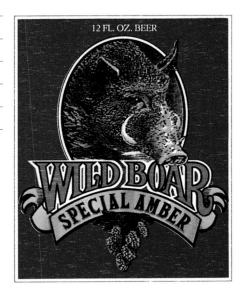

12 FL. OZ. BEER

WILD BOAR SPECIAL AMBER

Robert Imeson, the president of Dubuque, is a man divided.

"We're in the middle of the middle of the middle," he said of the brewery, which is in Dubuque—but whose headquarters are in Seattle. Not only is the company geographically split, but the brewery makes two different beers whose names aren't even in the same language. Simpatico, originally brewed in Mexico since 1986, is now bottled in Dubuque. So is Wild Boar. Nothing is simple.

But it is the Wild Boar beers that originated in the United States. Two Georgians, Bob Clark and Rob Nelson, created the recipes, and Dubuque decided to make them.

The **Wild Boar Special Amber** is a beautiful copper color, has a sweet malt aroma, and tastes crisp and hoppy. It is a perfectly presentable beer, whose offspring is **Wild Boar Winter Spiced.** "It's essentially the same recipe with a hundred pounds of chocolate malt thrown in, and nutmeg and cinnamon," Mr. Imeson said. And so it is.

RECOMMENDED: Wild Boar Special Amber
Wild Boar Winter Spiced

Eske's: A Brew Pub/ Sangre de Cristo Brewing

PO BOX 1572

106 DES GEORGES LANE

TAOS, NEW MEXICO 87571

PHONE: 505-758-1517

YEAR ESTABLISHED: 1992

In the world of American microbreweries, there are some distinct regional differences—hoppier in the West, sweeter in the South, lighter-bodied in the Midwest, and *hotter* in the Southwest.

Yes, hot as in chili beer.

Steve Eskeback, owner and brewmaster, whose nickname is Eske, brews one of the Southwest's chili beers, along with twenty-five other far more recognizable styles. At any given moment, six or seven are available, both on tap and hand-bottled (though bottles are available only on the premises). All are unpasteurized and unfiltered. In the springtime, Eskeback had five traditional beers: **10,000 Foot Stout, Mesa Pale Ale, Bert & Ernie Barley Wine, Scottish Ale,** and **Taos Mountain Gold.** The exotica were the **Taos Green Chili Beer** and a **Berry Beer,** made from blackberries, cherries, and raspberries.

To explore the beers, consider starting with the familiar and then moving on to the outer limits of taste. Know, too, that just as the owner goes by two names, so do his businesses. Eske gave one name to the brewpub and another to the company. "Sangre de Cristo Brewing Company has politically incorrect overtones," he said.

Mesa Pale Ale is a lively beer with a deep, hoppy flavor. The beer rolls around in the mouth, balanced and full-blown. But before you drink it, pour it into a glass and let the volatile, dry-hopped nose blow off so that it settles into a friendly, enticing aroma. Then drink.

When Eske started brewing, he was then living and working near the Taos Ski Valley, at the 10,000-foot level. So he named his Russian imperial stout for its birthplace.

Zesty and complex it is. Best, it smells as it looks and tastes, which is the definition of a cohesive beer. Rich and black, it has a highly chocolate nose with a hint of licorice and the same consistency in flavor.

Some people snort cocaine. To drink Taos Green Chili Beer is the equivalent of snorting hot green pepper. Eske roasts green chilis until the skins blacken, puts the whole chilis in a mesh bag, and the bag into the fermenting beer. For one week, the chilis do their pernicious work, and then they are discarded.

The beer smells and tastes of an incendiary green bell pepper. The nose (of the drinker, not the beer) heats up. The taste buds, if they could talk, say, *"What?!"*

A chili beer is perhaps something only a southwesterner

could love, just as thousand-year-old duck eggs are something that primarily only the Chinese adore. Chili beers are an acquired taste—not acquired here.

RECOMMENDED: **Mesa Pale Ale**
10,000 Foot Stout

F.X. Matt Brewing Company/Saranac

CONTRACT BREWER FOR NEW
AMSTERDAM, DOCK STREET,
AND OTHER COMPANIES

811 EDWARD ST.

UTICA, NEW YORK 13502

PHONE: 315-732-3181

YEAR ESTABLISHED: 1888

CAPACITY: 270,000 BARRELS.
NEARLY HALF THE CAPACITY IS
SARANAC, THE REMAINDER IS
CONTRACT BEERS.

F.X. Matt is the second oldest family-owned brewery in the United States, after Yuengling in Pottsville, Pennsylvania. But unlike some breweries, F.X. Matt does not claim to be brewing Grandpa's recipes, said president Nicholas (Nick) Matt.

It brews its beer according to the times. In 1888, it brewed under the West End Brewing Company name, at a time when there were ten breweries in Utica, ten in Syracuse, and three in Rome. F. X. (for Francis Xavier) Matt brewed until Prohibition, when he switched to malt tonic, malt syrup, and soft drinks, the latter under the Utica Club name. Hours after Prohibition ended on March 22, 1933, Matt was brewing beer again, this time under Utica Club. The name, of course, had instant recognition. Only the content of the bottle had changed.

Then the brewery made a near fatal mistake, introducing Matt's Premium, a mainstream beer, first in kegs, then in bottles. "We had some real difficulty in the '70s and '80s selling more mainstream beers," said Nick Matt. The family learned that they couldn't compete with the Big Three. "The national competitors lower their prices to a place where we can't make beer and make money," Mr. Matt said. "And on the other end of the spectrum, there's the advertising of Budweiser, Miller's, and Coors, which we can't possibly match."

What, then, was a brewery to do?

In 1982, Matt's began producing New Amsterdam, the first of many contract specialty beers. Also in the '80s, F. X. Matt II, Nick's brother and the current chairman and master brewer, created the recipe for **Saranac Adirondack Amber** and designed the other beers—**Saranac Black & Tan, Golden,** and **Pale Ale**—with others. In 1995, Matt is known both for contract brewing and for its Saranac beers.

Ask which companies it brews for, and Nick Matt is both discreet and polite. "I won't tell you the whole list," he said. "You say a name, and I won't deny it."

New Amsterdam?

Yes. Both draft and bottled.

Dock Street?

Yes. The bottled, and some draft.

If there is one word to describe the three Saranac beers, it may be *wholesome*. The beers are brewed with a sure, steady hand and can be drunk with ease, bottle after bottle—yet never startle nor offend.

If there is an all-American microbrewed pilsner, then **Saranac Golden Pilsener Beer** may be it. It is light, clean, and dry with a little spice at the finish.

Saranac Adirondack Amber is the beer equivalent to Calvin Klein clothing: consistent, clean, crisp, and not wildly exciting. Balance is pervasive, in the aroma and in the palate. It is a beer to count on, but not one to move the soul.

Saranac Black & Tan, a mix of dry Irish stout with an all-malt lager, is a beginner's stout. It has the chocolate, hoppy nose of a stout and introduces the unfamiliar to a deeper, darker brew. But although it is full-bodied, it doesn't have the full throttle of a stout. It's a stout to go with lunch, a green salad, or a plate of roasted peppers drizzled with olive oil. It's an early-in-the-day stout.

RECOMMENDED: **Saranac Golden Pilsener Beer**
Saranac Adirondack Amber
Saranac Black & Tan

Flat Branch Pub & Brewing Company

115 SOUTH FIFTH ST.

COLUMBIA, MISSOURI 65201

PHONE: 314-499-0400

YEAR ESTABLISHED: 1994

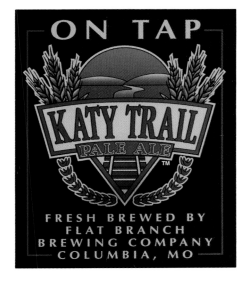

Marty Galloway is an engineer-turned-photographer-turned-brewmaster and co-owner of Flat Branch Pub & Brewing, which is named for the creek that runs behind the building. "In a strange kind of way, they're all intertwined," he said of his professions. "They're both mechanical and creative."

Year-round, he brews fourteen unpasteurized beers, which are available on tap, in growlers, and in kegs. But he hand-bottled three samples, and each arrived with flavor and carbonation intact. The brewery may be only one year old, but the beers aren't callow.

The **Katy Trail Pale Ale,** named for a hiking and biking trail that goes from St. Charles to Sedalia, is an India pale ale. Poured from a bottle, it must be drunk only after the carbon dioxide blows off. What's left is a well-balanced, well-hopped pale ale that has a nice aftertaste. "It's a perfect B plus beer," the beer consultant said.

The **Flat Branch Rye Ale** doesn't have an aftertaste, but the medium-bodied beer does have a malty, sweet, straight-ahead flavor.

Mr. Galloway doesn't always make an ordinary porter. He sometimes makes a **Smoked Porter,** using an imported peated malt that has already been smoked. Brewed as a dark beer, with chocolate and black patent malts, it has an even taste, neither sweet nor dry but in between. The brewmaster handles the peated malt with a careful, knowing hand. The smokiness is subtle and not overwhelming. The end result? A light porter that goes naturally and good-naturedly with food.

Mr. Galloway's springtime panoply of beers also includes **Tiger Tale Ale, Honey Wheaten,** a **Bitter, Scottish Ale, Irish Red Ale, Brown Ale, Dark Wheat, Market Square Stout, Weizenbock,** and **Green Chili Beer.** Perhaps chili beers are edging their way across state borders, moving sneakily in the night from the Southwest to the Midwest.

Perhaps chili beers should be quarantined.

RECOMMENDED: Katy Trail Pale Ale
Flat Branch Rye Ale
Flat Branch Smoked Porter

Fort Spokane Brewery Inc.

WEST 401 SPOKANE FALLS
   BOULEVARD

SPOKANE, WASHINGTON 99201

PHONE: 509-838-3809

YEAR ESTABLISHED: 1989

BREWED IN SPOKANE, WA 99201
1 QT.

At Fort Spokane, the **Border Run Ale,** a medium-bodied amber beer, is the flagship beer, the favorite of both the public and one of the owners. Dean Davis, a partner, assistant manager, and self-described "Head Beer-taster," said the beer was complex, with a slightly bitter edge to it, without being too aggressive. It is as he says.

There's a lovely fresh aroma, a faint caramel maltiness, a bit of hop, and an equally fresh tastiness. It's a pert beer.

Year-round, the brewery also offers a **Blond Alt,** a **Red Alt,** a **Bulldog Stout,** and assorted seasonal beers.

RECOMMENDED: **Fort Spokane Border Run Ale**

Full Sail Brewing Co.

506 COLUMBIA ST.

HOOD RIVER, OREGON 97031

PHONE: 541-386-2281

YEAR ESTABLISHED: 1987

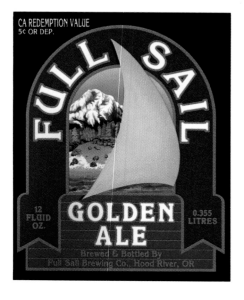

I'm a *zealot!*" said Jerome Chicvara, a partner and the sales manager for Full Sail. In his life, there are a few certainties: death, taxes, and the joy of drinking at least two (if he's driving) or three twelve-ounce bottles of beer each day. His enthusiasm for beer is unbridled—and also focused.

Chicvara doesn't love just the taste, flavor, color, and smell of beer. He is also a beer visionary who foresees a world where people are so enamored, or even awash, in microbrewed beers that they will flock to microbreweries as destination points, just like vacationers go to Disneyland.

And who will be there to greet them?

Jerome Chicvara.

"Visit the well! Smell the hops! Sit down at my bar! Come to my brewery!"

He wants Full Sail to be like Redhook Ale Brewery in Seattle. Anheuser-Busch bought a minority share in Redhook, and both the big and little breweries profited. When A-B became a part of the microbrewery movement, Redhook not only expanded but also gained access to A-B's extraordinary distribution network.

Chicvara raved about Redhook's newest facility in Woodinville, Washington. "It cost fourteen million dollars! It's got nature trails! Duck ponds! Concerts!"

Asked if he was jealous, he said, "I can be jealous or I can ask, 'How can *I* do this?'

"We've met with Miller, Seagram's, Coors," Chicvara added. "We want two hundred million dollars." In the ideal world, "We would still make the beer, and they'd be paying our pay checks," he said. So far, there have been no takers.

As for young people who want to leap into microbrewing, Chicvara has this advice: "Open a brewpub, not a brewery. Where you brew, a pint of beer is 700 percent markup. A pint that sells for three dollars costs fifty cents to make," he said. "To open a brewery, you need a two-million-dollar bottling line and trucks. For a brewpub, you can buy used restaurant supplies and get clean glasses and clean lines."

Full Sail does both—bottles and has a brewpub. Year-round, Full Sail brews thirteen beers, including an imperial porter, and bottles three—an amber, a gold, and a pilsner. What the company refuses to brew are berry beers and wheat beers.

Full Sail Amber Ale, the best-seller, accounts for 50 percent of sales, Mr. Chicvara said. It has an enticing malty aroma, and a hint of caramel in the tasting.

A gentle beer is **Full Sail Golden Ale,** the second-best-selling style. It is mild-mannered in every sense. Both hops and malts are present in a benign, nonassertive fashion. It starts with a mild sweetness but finishes mildly dry. "It's a little bit fuller than a quaffing beer," the beer consultant said.

The tastiest beer is the **Full Sail Pilsner.** Made with traditional Czechoslovakian Saaz hops, it is bright, crisp, and clear. The expected bitterness comes on in the flavor and lingers in the mouth. A smooth, refreshing beer, it makes no creative detours but is delectably true to type.

RECOMMENDED: Full Sail Pilsner
Full Sail Amber Ale
Full Sail Golden Ale

Great Basin Brewing Company

846 VICTORIAN AVE.

SPARKS, NEVADA 89431

PHONE: 702-355-7711

YEAR ESTABLISHED: 1993

The mainstream beer drinker says, "Gimme a Bud!"

The Great Basin fan says, "Gimme an Icky!"

What he'll get is the **Ichthyosaur IPA,** an India pale ale named for a seafaring dinosaur whose fossils are found in Nevada. It is one of four beers brewed by Tom Young, the brewmaster and a co-owner. Along with the Icky, Mr. Young brews a **Wild Horse Ale,** a **Nevada Gold,** and a **Jackpot Porter.**

The company, which sells bottles only from bars, is named for a geological region where the rivers drain into the Great Basin, Mr. Young said.

The Jackpot Porter survived its cross-country jaunt and revealed itself to possess a nice, roasted, cocoa nose and a sweetish flavor. Its robustness, however, was lost en route.

RECOMMENDED: Great Basin Jackpot Porter

The Great Lakes Brewing Co.

2516 MARKET AVE.

CLEVELAND, OHIO 44113

PHONE: 216-771-4404

FAX: 216-771-4466

YEAR ESTABLISHED: 1988

CAPACITY: 16,000 BARRELS

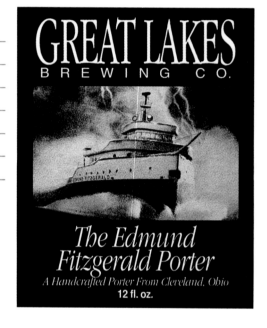

GREAT LAKES
B R E W I N G   C O.

The Edmund Fitzgerald Porter
A Handcrafted Porter From Cleveland, Ohio
12 fl. oz.

To read the labels of Great Lakes' beers is to be a tourist. Two beers are named for local heroes, two for local disasters.

If Americans were to free-associate the name Eliot Ness, some would mumble FBI. Moviegoers would say Kevin Costner *as* Eliot Ness in the film *The Untouchables*. But to Clevelanders, Ness was once their safety director, and to Patrick and Dan Conway, the owners of Great Lakes Brewing Company, Ness was a beer drinker who emptied his pints at the bar that is part of their building. So, to commemorate their famous patron, the Conways created **The Eliot Ness**

Vienna Styled Lager, whose label reads: "For flavor and freshness, The Eliot Ness is untouchable."

It has a delicate, floral bouquet, an upfront maltiness, and a nice medium-bodied mouth feel. The finish is appealingly bitter.

Consider the name John D. Rockefeller. Standard Oil? Rockefeller Center? Zillions of dollars? All that and more. He also had an accounting office in the Conways' building, and, like Ness, has been immortalized in a beer.

The Rockefeller Bock has the color of mahogany, is roasty and chocolaty, and tastes like a lovely, light stout.

The Edmund Fitzgerald Porter is named for a ship that used Cleveland as its home port and sank in 1979—with Clevelanders on board. "It was the largest ship on the Great Lakes, and traveled back and forth with raw materials for the steel mills," said Patrick Conway.

To taste the beer is to discover a porter with training wheels. It is a tasty, although light porter, with a roasty, chocolaty flavor.

Burning River Pale Ale commemorates the moment when the Cuyahoga River caught fire and burned the bridge down, Mr. Conway said. It is a proper pale ale with a malty nose and a full hoppy flavor that lingers.

"**The Dortmunder Gold** is the only name that has no real connection to us," Mr. Conway said. Golden in color, the lager is more sweet than malty, but is nicely balanced with an almost honeyed flavor.

From this highly consistent brewery, there are also **The Moon Dog Ale,** an **Oktoberfest,** and a **Christmas Ale.**

RECOMMENDED: Great Lakes The Edmund Fitzgerald Porter
Great Lakes Burning River Pale Ale
Great Lakes The Eliot Ness Vienna Styled Lager
Great Lakes The Rockefeller Bock
Great Lakes Dortmunder Gold

Gritty McDuff's Brewing Company

369 FORE ST.

PORTLAND, MAINE 04101

PHONE: 207-772-2739

BOTTLED BEER IS CONTRACT-
BREWED AT THE GEARY
BREWING COMPANY

PORTLAND, MAINE

YEAR ESTABLISHED: 1988

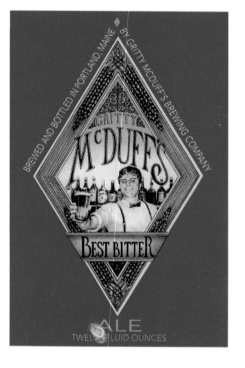

Secretly, I always wanted to be a brewmaster," said Ed Stebbins, owner and head brewer, "but I didn't come out of the closet until I was twenty-five. Nobody took me seriously."

In 1988, he opened Gritty McDuff's, a brewpub, where he serves what he calls Americanized pub grub: fish and chips, steak and kidney pie, hamburger, and, in the summertime, sweet, luscious lobsters.

It is the definition of gustatory heaven to eat a freshly boiled lobster (or a lobster roll) with an ice cold bottle of beer. The hoppiness of the beer is a crisp counterpoint to the sweet richness of the lobster. **Gritty McDuff's Best Bitter** is a perfect accompaniment. It has a subtle floral nose, a beautifully balanced palate, a round mouth feel, and a good hop character. It is a fulsome beer.

Gritty McDuff's Best Brown is a deceptive beer. It smells like it will be sweet and treacly, but reveals itself to be a somewhat thin, hoppy beer whose floral notes come on stronger, later. It's a beer that probably thrives best when served not ice cold. Think British. Think just slightly warm.

RECOMMENDED: Gritty McDuff's Best Bitter

air of the Dog Brewing Company, Inc.

4509 S.E. 23RD ST.

PORTLAND, OREGON 97202

PHONE: 503-232-6585

YEAR ESTABLISHED: 1994

We're nutty," said Doug Henderson, who, with Alan Sprintz, owns what may be America's smallest and most exotic microbrewery.

They brew only two bottle-conditioned beers that are designed either to be drunk immediately or to be laid down and drunk in two to ten years. Just as there are signed editions of art, Hair of the Dog has signed batches of beer, with each week's batch of three thousand getting a different number.

The brewery itself is so far removed from the center of Portland that the owners/brewers fax maps to anyone planning to visit them. They named the brewery after the old wives' tale that to cure a dog bite, you take the hair of the dog that bit you, make a poultice over the wound, and put the hair in the poultice. "The phrase 'hair of the dog' meant a cure for a hangover," Mr. Henderson said.

To properly inaugurate the brewery, the owners decided they needed a live dog to make its contribution. Since the man who was pouring the concrete floor just happened to have his dog along, the owners borrowed the canine and ceremoniously plopped its paws into the wet cement.

With all this effort to make Hair of the Dog unlike any other American brewery, what are the beers like?

Golden Rose: A Belgian Triple Style Ale is a homage to Portland, which is also known as the city of roses. The name is also a way to appeal to anyone who might judge a beer by its label. "It's a pretty name," Mr. Henderson said.

It's also a pretty beer, luscious in fact. It's a winey beer, with a malty sweetness balanced by a subtle hoppiness. For an additional note of sweetness, the brewers toss in white rock candy. The special winey character makes the Golden Rose a perfect accompaniment to a choucroute or a platter of ripe cheeses.

The **Adambier,** a revival of a very strong, rich, dark ale once brewed in Dortmund, has its fans and detractors. Its alcoholic strength is 8 percent by weight, which is twice the strength of an ordinary beer. It is sweet and treacly, which for some makes it the beer equivalent of a dessert wine—to be poured frugally and sipped very, very leisurely. For others, it is far too sweet to be palatable. It does, however, age nicely. A batch marked #9, which meant it was two months old when tasted, was intensely sweet. But batch #1, which when tasted was ten months old, had a sharpness to the bittering.

It is a controversial beer. Your choice.

RECOMMENDED: **Golden Rosebier**

The Hangtown Brewery

2805 MALLARD LANE, NO. 1

PLACERVILLE, CALIFORNIA 95667

PHONE: 916-621-3999

YEAR ESTABLISHED: 1992

CAPACITY: 7,200 BARRELS

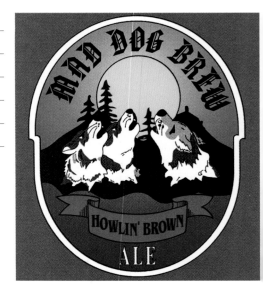

The gold rush of the 1840s commenced just eight miles north of Placerville, California. Fifty miles to the east the pony express was born. And in the town of Placerville itself, several men were once hanged from an old oak tree, giving the burg its somewhat notorious nickname, "Hangtown."

In 1992, in his five-hundred-square-foot shop in Placerville, David Coody, the brewmaster (and one of Hangtown's major stockholders), bottled his first case of pale ale, then sold the twenty-four bottles for $2 each. He was tiptoeing into the market.

"People said, 'Yeah, I'd like some more,'" said Matthew Chitiea, corporate secretary of the brewery. And so, on that small but auspicious note, Hangtown Brewery was born.

Called **Hangtown Pale Ale,** the flagship beer tastes like an

India pale ale, overly hopped for some taste buds and reasonably hopped for others. The nose is also subject to quibble. Some said it smelled of green hops, others of stale hops. It is an imperfect but drinkable beer.

Mad Dog Brew Howlin' Brown Ale is a mouthful of a name for a hybrid beer. Stylistically, it hovers between a porter and a brown ale. It has the roasty, chocolate nose and flavor of a porter but a lighter body than a porter.

Year-round, the brewery also makes a **Strong Blond, Summer Ale, Boysenberry Ale,** and **Stout.** To celebrate the seasons, there are **Allspice Ale, Green Irish Ale,** and **Tangerine Ale.**

RECOMMENDED: Mad Dog Brew Howlin' Brown Ale

H art Brewing, Inc./ Pyramid Breweries Inc.

91 SOUTH ROYAL BROUGHAM WAY

SEATTLE, WASHINGTON 98134

PHONE: 206-682-8322

FAX: 206-682-8420

ALSO INCORPORATING PYRAMID ALES IN KALAMA, WASHINGTON, AND BERKELEY, CALIFORNIA, AND THOMAS KEMPER LAGERS IN POULSBO, WASHINGTON

YEAR ESTABLISHED: 1984

CAPACITY: 170,000 BARRELS

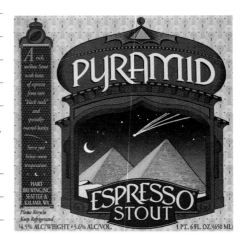

Is the Pope Catholic?

Are Washingtonians hopheads?

The answer to both questions is yes.

But the reason Washingtonians drink hoppy beers is simple. Seventy-three percent of the hops grown in the United States are from Washington State, primarily in and around the Yakima Valley.

Rande Reed, the brewmaster, said there are gender differences in why people go to brewpubs like Hart's. "When there's a couple, the man is looking for a distinct, more adventurous beer," Mr. Reed said, "and the woman is coming along because the guy wants to go to a brewpub."

Some beers are more adventurous than others. **Pyramid Espresso Stout** has the classic seductive aroma of espresso coffee tinged with chocolate and a flavor that is not quite as rich, dense, or textured as promised. Still, it is a delectable, well-brewed stout.

Pyramid Pale Ale has depth. The amber beer has a dense, hoppy aroma, and is a fat, full-bodied beer with a complex caramel-malt flavor—and a hoppy finish and aftertaste.

For those who like to drink their bread, there is the **Pyramid Hefeweizen,** whose yeasty aroma nearly overpowers the very mild flavor. In the world of wheat beers, Pierre Celis may make the most exotic and addictive version in the United States, but Pyramid made the first, in 1984, Mr. Reed said.

"Hybrid" best describes the **Pyramid Amber Wheat Beer.** It is as if the brewers asked themselves, what's popular? Amber. And? Wheat.

So let's mix the two.

It is hoppier and tastier than a wheat beer on its own, but it has a wheat beer's faint citric quality. Some would say it was neither here nor there, but somewhere in between.

The **Pyramid Apricot Ale** is mystifying. It has won awards, and is tangy, effervescent, and gently perfumed. But it is so light as to be ephemeral. It seems to be a beer one could serve to a minor.

The **Pyramid Best Brown Ale** went thin, acrid, and musty. Perhaps it was a bad bottle.

From Thomas Kemper, the **Dark Lager** had a faint nose, a proper malty/hoppy balance in the flavor, but then vanished without a trace—or, rather, a taste. "No follow-through," someone said.

Whatever personality the **Thomas Kemper Gold Lager** had disappeared as the bottle was opened and went funky in both the sour smell and taste.

The three breweries also make seasonal ales and lagers, and, in the way of food, the brewpub offers addictive baby-back ribs glossed with an Espresso Stout Barbecue Sauce.

RECOMMENDED: Pyramid Espresso Stout
Pyramid Pale Ale

Humboldt Brewing Company

856 10TH ST.

ARCATA, CALIFORNIA 95521-9016

PHONE: 707-826-2739

YEAR ESTABLISHED: 1987

BREWED & BOTTLED BY
HUMBOLDT BREWING COMPANY
ARCATA, CALIFORNIA

We're kind of small," said Steve Parkes, the English head brewer of Humboldt, which is tucked away in the middle of Redwood National Park. Although the brewery may be dwarfed by the immense ancient trees, this is not to say that Humboldt's beers are insignificant. The clue to enjoying the beers is to wait until they blow off and then, and only then, imbibe.

The **Gold Nectar Ale** is so floral it smells like a woman wearing too much perfume. So relax, let the aromas vanish into the air, and then taste the medium-bodied, slightly spicy beer. It is palatable.

The **Red Nectar Ale** has a similar body but is a darker, coppery color, with more malty flavor, more depth, and more cohesiveness. It is the better of the two beers.

RECOMMENDED: Red Nectar Ale

Irons Brewing Company

12354 WEST ALAMEDA PARKWAY, UNIT E

LAKEWOOD, COLORADO 80228

PHONE: 303-985-2337

YEAR ESTABLISHED: 1992

Some of the labels have the strange, haunted look of the artwork for *Dungeons and Dragons*. Supernal beasts. Ferocious knights with magical swords. Landscapes covered by unnatural mists, sheltered by pink-hued skies. The labels, then, are an overwrought buildup for some decent beers and simultaneously immortalize the president and brewmaster, Larry Irons. Every beer has the word *iron* in its name.

Long Iron Bohemian Style Pilsner Beer is a medium-bodied beer with a small nose and an appealing, crisp, well-balanced palate. It is totally refreshing and extremely easy to like.

Iron Heart Red Ale has a neutral malty sweetness, first revealed in the nose, and then sustained throughout. The hoppiness is so mild as to be almost undetectable.

American Iron Amber Ale is a better-balanced beer than the Iron Heart Red Ale.

There are one-note songs, and **Dark Iron Chocolate Brown Ale** is a one-flavor beer. The taste of chocolate explodes in the mouth, then dwindles away. The beer lacks nuances.

For dessert, skip the pie, the cake, and the crème brûlée. Consider instead **Winter Iron Bock Beer,** a round, medium-bodied, strong, malty beer.

There is also **Grid Iron Oktoberfest Style Lager.**

RECOMMENDED: Long Iron Bohemian Style Pilsner Beer
American Iron Amber Ale
Winter Iron Bock Beer

The Jasper Murdock Alehouse at the Norwich Inn

PO BOX 908

MAIN ST.

NORWICH, VERMONT 05055

PHONE: 802-649-1143

YEAR ESTABLISHED: 1993

The NORWICH INN

ESTABLISHED 1797

WHISTLING PIG RED ALE

BREWED AND BOTTLED ON PREMISES BY
THE NORWICH INN
NORWICH, VERMONT

Here is a trade secret.

Some of the most delectable microbrewed beers in America are at the Jasper Murdock Alehouse. Brewed solely as an amenity for guests to the Norwich Inn, the beers, which are available only on tap (but which were hand-bottled and sent to Manhattan) are superb.

In 1991, Sally Wilson bought the inn, which dates from 1797, and two years later her husband, Tim Wilson, began to offer eleven beers. Three are on tap at any time.

He has the gift.

The **Short 'n' Stout** is all things wonderful. Touted as a dry

Irish stout, it has a toasty aroma, heady with chocolate, and a perfectly balanced and intense flavor of sweetness and bitterness. It rolls around the tongue, deep, dark and luscious. Even its name—in honor of the inn's mascot, a Welsh corgi named Jasper Murdock—is memorable.

The most popular beer, **Whistling Pig Red Ale,** has a lovely garnet color, a faint nose, and a rounded, malty flavor that finishes with a lingering hoppy aftertaste. Each year, on Groundhog Day, there is a local Whistling Pig Game dinner—hence the name of the ale.

The definition of an extra special bitter is that it is well hopped. But it is Tim Wilson's deft hand that reveals **Jasper Murdock's Extra Special Bitter** to have its hoppiness show up at the end, at the very back of the mouth—and linger.

Some of his other (and untasted) beers have straightforward names, and some do not.

There are **Elijah Burton's Mild Ale,** named for the man who cleared the site of the inn, and **Dr. Bowles' Honey Elixir,** a pale ale named for the innkeeper who in 1889 saw the inn burn down—and rebuilt it. **Stackpole Porter** honors James Stackpole, an ancestor of Tim Wilson's who, in 1693, had a public house that sold beer cider, and rum. Long ago in Vermont, there was a legendary bear that was so strong he could squeeze sap from the biggest maple trees. For him, there is **Old Slipperyskin India Pale Ale.**

In the category of silly names, there are **Fuggle & Barleycorn,** named (respectively) for the English hop and the barley malt that go into this pale ale. **O.B. Joyful** is what Vermont's soldiers in the Civil War called any drink they fermented from hardtack or other provisions. **Bronx Cheer the Raspberry Beer** is, in a wiseass fashion, a beer that incorporates fresh raspberries. **Heifer Vice Wheat Beer** is a pun on the Bavarian hefeweiss.

RECOMMENDED: Whistling Pig Red Ale
Jasper Murdock's Extra Special Bitter
Short 'n' Stout

Kennebunkport Brewing Co. & Shipyard Brewing Company

NO. 86 NEWBURY ST.

PORTLAND, MAINE 04101

PHONE: 207-761-0807

FAX: 207-775-5567

YEAR ESTABLISHED: 1992

Old **Thumper Extra Special Ale** is (thankfully?) not named for a pet.

Alan Pugsley, the English head brewer and co-owner, tells the story of how Old Thumper got its name. In 1982, he first learned to brew it at Ringwood Brewery in Hampshire, England, and now makes it through a licensing agreement with Ringwood. But when the ale was first brewed, it was called the No-Name Bitter. Ringwood sponsored a radio contest in which listeners were invited to give it a name. One man drank too much of it, woke up the next morning with a thumping headache, submitted the name "Old Thumper"—and won. That was his glimpse of immortality.

For those who drink beer to satisfy an alcoholic sweet tooth, Old Thumper is the right beer. The company says it's an untraditional English bitter, and where it departs from the standard is that if it is highly hopped (as bitters are supposed to be), the palate doesn't detect it.

Amber in color, the ale has a nose that doesn't jump, but quietly insinuates itself with fruity aromas and has a sweet, malty taste on the tongue. The beer is consistent in that it delivers what it promises, but it is too sweet to refresh.

Not so **The Shipyard Export Ale,** the flagship beer. It is highly tasty, richly colored, and memorable. The color is a deep gold verging to amber. The nose is hoppy, there is an upfront maltiness, a smoothly balanced flavor, and a very dry but not too bitter finish. The ale has depth.

So does **The Shipyard Blue Fin Stout.** It is a dry Irish stout with an enticing dark black color and a creamy head. "It pours thick and tastes full," Mr. Pugsley said. Stouts are made to be inhaled, and the nose has the classic chocolate and coffee notes—and a bit of burned sugar. It is not at all sweet but pleasingly dry to the palate.

The Shipyard Moose Brown Ale is to beers what herbal teas are to teas. The ale has a hoppy nose that turns spicy, herbal, sweet, and flowery in the mouth.

The truth about most light beers is that they often have fewer calories and, as an organic consequence, usually deserve fewer words. **The Shipyard Goat Island Light Ale,** at 110 calories per ten-ounce serving, is no exception. The calorie-watcher's beer, its greatest asset is the faint balanced nose that is more sensual than the bland, inconsequential flavor.

RECOMMENDED: The Shipyard Export Ale
                             The Shipyard Blue Fin Stout

The Left Hand Brewing Company, Ltd.

1265 BOSTON AVE.

LONGMONT, COLORADO 80501

PHONE: 303-772-0258

YEAR ESTABLISHED: 1994

CAPACITY: 5,000 BARRELS

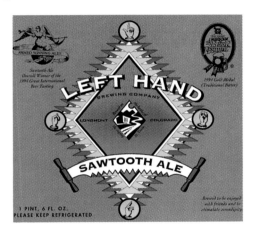

Left Hand Brewing is young, small, and still struggling.

At best, its beers are hopeful.

Dick Doors and Eric Wallace, the co-owners, brewers, and Air Force Academy graduates, have given the beers a distinct Southwest image. The name is taken from Chief Niwot, a Southern Arapaho Indian who once spent winters in the Boulder Valley and whose name translates to "Left Hand." The logo, which resembles a sawtooth-edged Native American rug, was inspired by a mountain that Mr. Doors can see each morning when he looks out his bedroom window. Its name is Sawtooth.

The labels are more sophisticated than the beers.

The **Left Hand Sawtooth Ale** is a deep amber English bitter with clear malty notes but very little hoppiness.

The **Left Hand Motherlode Golden Ale** smells fruity and tastes biscuity—or yeasty.

Being young (Doors is thirty-two, and Wallace is thirty-three) and experimental, the two brewers have taken ginger, an ancient bittering agent, to make the very light, aromatic **Juju Ginger,** an ale brewed with the freshly ground, unpeeled root. It smells of the ginger, and tastes of the ginger—a novelty beer. But Left Hand has found its customers—Asian restaurants, especially sushi bars. "It's a niche we weren't expecting to hit," Mr. Doors said.

The Juju Ginger is proof that there is a beer for everyone, no matter how quaint the taste.

RECOMMENDED: Left Hand Sawtooth Ale

Lost Coast Brewery & Cafe

617 FOURTH ST.

EUREKA, CALIFORNIA 95501

PHONE: 707-445-4480

FAX: 707-445-4483

YEAR ESTABLISHED: 1990

CAPACITY: 4,000 BARRELS

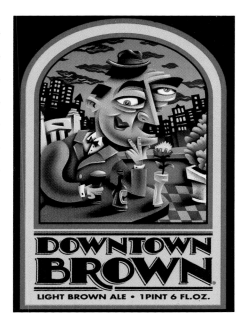

One day in the late '80s, Barbara Groom, a bored pharmacist, walked into the Mendocino Brewing Company in Hopland, California—and was transfigured. She was bitten by the brew bug.

She had seen the future, and it was brewing. She read Charlie Papazian's book, *The Complete Joy of Home Brewing,* bought home-brewing equipment, and took microbiology classes at the University of California at Davis. Armed with this smattering of knowledge, she home-brewed twenty batches of beer and bought the brewery (with co-owner Wendy Pound).

"The first batch was good," Ms. Groom said, "and I never turned back." Fearless, she also commissioned Duane Flatmo, a local artist who works in a bizarre cubist style, to design some of the labels.

The art is strange and tortured; the beers are not.

Downtown Brown Light Brown Ale, the flagship beer, has a tiny malty nose, a mild flavor, and no aftertaste. It is a small, drinkable beer.

Alleycat Amber Ale is a slightly pallid beer whose hoppiness is barely discernible. It is a beer for the timorous.

These two beers, however, are only part of the offerings. Year-round, there are **Lost Coast Pale Ale, Black Vulture Stout, Ol' Thrasher Wheat Ale,** and **Chocolate Raspberry Brown Ale.** The seasonal bottled beer is **Winterbraun Holiday Ale.**

As one of the few women brewmasters in the United States, Ms. Groom is sanguine.

"The only drawback of brewing is having to work with men," she said. "They are a different animal. They have the 'good old boy' network. No matter how liberated they are, they still look down on women."

She has five men working for her as assistant brewers, cellar rats, and the bottling crew. "They do pretty good, taking orders from me," said Ms. Groom, who is forty-seven. "But I would *love* to have an all-women brewery!"

RECOMMENDED: Downtown Brown Light Brown Ale

agic Hat Brewing Co.

180 FLYNN AVE.

BURLINGTON, VERMONT 05401

PHONE: 802-658-2739

FAX: 802-658-5788

YEAR ESTABLISHED: 1994

Alan Newman, president and, with Bob Johnson, the brew-master, a co-owner of the Magic Hat Brewing Co., predicts the future of microbreweries by paraphrasing Buckminster Fuller:

"There are rules on how the universe works. Bigger, bigger, bigger, smaller. Everything, whether it's an electronic device, or a car, or an industry, gets bigger, bigger, and bigger, and then at some point, it transforms, and gets real small," he said.

Microbreweries are no longer rare. By Newman's figures, in 1900 there were 2,000 breweries in the United States, which dwindled to 231 in the depression and 82 in 1980, when many breweries consolidated. Now, there are around 500.

"In five years, the large breweries, the Big Three, are going to own 50 to 60 percent of the microbreweries, and will control distribution, and therefore [control] the beer industry once again—and somebody will start franchising the pub system," Mr. Newman said. "But there will be a group of micros who will do things unusually, who will continue to innovate."

Magic Hat, he said, will *not* be bought.

The flagship beer is the only year-round beer: **Magic Hat Ale.** Styled as an Irish red ale, it has a reddish amber color, a splendidly fresh, hoppy nose, and a smooth, creamy-malty flavor and a spicy, nonsweet finish. As someone said, "Take off your magic hat to them." It is an excellent beer.

The summer seasonal is #9, and it is a dubious beer. Called **Not Quite Pale Ale,** it smells like peaches and cloves. Sniffing it is like opening a fashion magazine and an unwanted fruity fragrance wafts into the air. Consider it an experiment.

RECOMMENDED: Magic Hat Ale

Maritime Pacific Brewing Co.

PO BOX 17812

SEATTLE, WASHINGTON 98107

PHONE: 206-782-6181

YEAR ESTABLISHED: 1990

CAPACITY: 5,000 BARRELS

George Hancock had his midlife epiphany at a brewpub. At the age of forty, he quit his job at an engineering company, hired on as a bartender at Noggin's, a Seattle brewpub, and saw the future.

It was a brewery. "I didn't want the hassle of a restaurant," he said. Neither does he care about getting rich. His focus is the local market. In 1992, there were sixteen breweries in Washington, he said. By 1995, there were forty-five. "Recognition is the key," said Mr. Hancock, who, with his wife, Jane, lived on a sailboat for fourteen years and named his brewery after their love for the sea. He works nearly seven days a week—and is a tired but happy man.

Maritime Flagship Red Ale is a true Irish red ale, with a proper malty nose, a medium body, and a greater emphasis on the malt than on the hop.

Maritime Nightwatch has a roasty, caramel nose and the expected maltiness, enhanced with a little bit of spice. It is the best of the three. **Maritime Pacific Islander Pale** is a light, malty beer with a very abrupt finish.

Mr. Hancock also brews a **Salmon Bay Bitter** and **Jolly Rogers,** a Christmas ale.

In Seattle, a city where people aspire to a laid-back style (both in conversational tone and mode of attire) and just hate to say bad things about each other (even if they're livid), the Hancocks have an annual rite of friendliness between them and their customers.

It's a pig roast.

Each summer, in the yard behind the brewery, the Hancocks roast four pigs at 200° for twelve hours in ovens they built themselves. To watch over the pigs, the Hancocks sleep out in the yard. Asked if the skin of the roasted pigs is golden and crackling, Mr. Hancock said, "No. It comes out black, and we peel it off."

The four hundred to five hundred guests apparently don't mind. Such is the style in Seattle.

RECOMMENDED: Maritime Pacific Nightwatch
Maritime Pacific Flagship Red Ale

Mass. Bay Brewing Co., Inc.

306 NORTHERN AVE.

BOSTON, MASSACHUSETTS 02210

PHONE: 617-574-9551

FAX: 617-574-9551 EXT. 4

YEAR ESTABLISHED: 1987

CAPACITY: 40,000 BARRELS

BOTTLED BEER IS CONTRACTED TO
F.X. MATT BREWING COMPANY,
UTICA, NEW YORK

In the late nineteenth century, in the time of Henry James, cultured young Americans traveled to Europe for art and culture. They lurked in museums, they haunted cathedrals. Girls yearned to marry royalty. So did boys. In the late twentieth century, young, curious Americans continue to go to Europe, not just in pursuit of high culture but in pursuit of great beers. The yearning is to marry American ingenuity with European beer styles. In beer lies romance.

Richard Doyle, president of the Mass. Bay Brewing Co., and his partners had their beer awakening in Europe and now make four year-round beers and four seasonals.

Harpoon Light is as its name says: light. At 115 calories, it has a little toast in the aroma and a little malt in the palate.

The **Harpoon Ale** is a deceptive beer. It is more expressive in the mouth than the nose. It starts off with a very genteel, even shy nose, and then opens up into a full-bodied, fruity, malty ale that ends with a soft bite.

Harpoon Stout, the spring seasonal, has the anticipated roasty, chocolate hoppy nose, and tastes more like a well-made, slightly dry porter than a full-blown stout.

RECOMMENDED: Harpoon Ale
Harpoon Stout

M cNeill's Brewery

90 ELLIOTT ST.

BRATTLEBORO, VERMONT 05301

PHONE: 802-254-2553

YEAR ESTABLISHED: 1991

By his own admission, when Ray McNeill started making his own beers in 1991, the owner and brewmaster was "relatively clueless."

He's clueless no longer. Year-round, he brews eight ales and makes twenty-two seasonal beers, from a pilsner to an imperial stout. Most of the beers have silly names, but the beers themselves are seldom silly. They're traditional styles, brewed true to type.

The label of **Big Nose Blond Ale** depicts a lion, which makes the name of the beer even more of a non sequitur. But the beer is a well-made, light pale ale with character. The color is a pale gold, and the beer opens with a clean, fresh nose, then merrily rolls around in the mouth, revealing a nice understated bitterness and a little floral note.

Firehouse Amber Ale starts off malty and creamy, and segues into hoppiness. It is a decent beer.

Name a beer **Duck's Breath Ale** and you are asking for quips.

"I've never kissed a duck," someone said as he was about to sniff the beer.

"I'd *rather* kiss a duck," said another after he inhaled the aroma. It is a curious beer whose nose does not bode well. Although the aroma of a beer is only part of its personality, it can be alluring or off-putting. The beer has a funky, barnyard smell, but if you can work through the nose and plunge into the beer itself, the palate is well balanced, although neutral.

Professor Brewhead's Brown Ale has no mixed signals. It smells like a malty brown ale with a whiff of chocolate, a creamy head, and a nicely balanced, low-keyed dry taste. It tastes as it should.

The beer consultant poured the **Pullman's Porter,** and the foam rose and rose until it was three inches high. Then it sat there. "A fobby beer," he said, using the English word for "foamy."

He then commanded the tasters to write our initials in the foam with our fingers. If the head stayed firm, as he anticipated, we would be able to read our initials in the foam, even as we got down to the very last sip.

The beer was flawless. It smelled like a roasty coffee cappuccino with notes of chocolate. Someone thought it was overly hopped, but others violently disagreed. It was lighter than it looked, and very addictive.

At the end, as we stared at the bottom of our glasses, what did we see?

Our initials.

"The foam has memory," someone said.

Dead Horse India Pale Ale has the same problem Duck's Breath Ale had—a funky nose, but a tasty palate. It is heavily hopped, nicely malty, well balanced—and true to style.

RECOMMENDED: Big Nose Blond Ale
Professor Brewhead's Brown Ale
Pullman's Porter

Mendocino Brewing Co.

HOPLAND BREWERY

13351 SOUTH HIGHWAY

PO BOX 400

HOPLAND, CALIFORNIA 95449

PHONE: 707-744-1015

YEAR ESTABLISHED: 1983

Mendocino! You've gotta try Mendocino!" said Bill ("I don't want lunch! I want BEER!") Owens.

He was right. The beers are complex, seductive, and delicious. Even the logo is exquisite. The design is an oval, embellished with barley, surrounding a cluster of hops. Rarely can you judge a beer by its label, but Mendocino is an exception.

Blue Heron Pale Ale has a classic, understated fruity nose and a splendidly rich palate: fresh, hoppy, slightly floral, and well balanced. Even the aftertaste is right. "It lingers ten seconds," someone said. "Like a good guest, it knows when to leave."

Red Tail Ale is perfect, in another way. It has spice, balance, and an underlying fruitiness, and finishes with a dry aftertaste.

Black Hawk Stout is what the Irish want stout to be. It has a very dark, roasty, chocolate nose and tastes smooth and rich, but not heavy. As an Irish architect said, "This is the kind of stout that in Ireland, a man huddles up to you and says, pointing to his pint, 'This is lunch.' "

Mendocino also makes **Peregrine Pale Ale** and opened California's first brewpub since Prohibition.

What it does best, however, is make wonderful beers—consistently.

RECOMMENDED: Blue Heron Pale Ale
Red Tale Ale
Black Hawk Stout

Libertyville Brewing Company d/b/a

MICKEY FINN'S BREWERY

412 N. MILWAUKEE AVE.

LIBERTYVILLE, ILLINOIS 60048

PHONE: 708-362-6688

YEAR ESTABLISHED: 1994

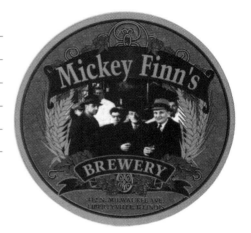

Ninety-five percent of the people who come in here have never had anything but Bud or Miller," said Christopher Swersey, the brewmaster. Given the innocence of the customers, the brewpub's flagship beer is also its lightest: **Whitetail Wheat Ale.** "It's our training-wheel beer," Mr. Swersey said.

But it is not his only beer. He has five to seven beers on tap at all times and sends them out in growlers, both locally and across the country, when asked. Along with Whitetail, he makes an **Abana Amber Ale,** a **Pale Ale, Five Springs Oatmeal Stout,** and other seasonals.

Mickey Finn's Pale Ale pours right. Its full head sits there, unperturbed, settled in and inviting. An aroma wafts up, and it is slightly malty, slightly hoppy—but not *too* hoppy. The flavor is as promised: beautifully balanced, full-bodied, and, on afterthought, engagingly dry.

In Libertyville, which is forty miles north of Chicago and fifty miles south of Milwaukee, there are at least five sulfur springs that supposedly had medicinal value. "There's a local Indian legend that each of the five springs cured a different illness—arthritis, respiratory illness," Mr. Swersey said.

Although **Mickey Finn's Five Springs Oatmeal Stout** isn't expected to cure any illness, it will satisfy a craving for a perfect stout.

Made with more than 15 percent rolled oats, the stout has the proper huge, creamy head. Sniff the roasted aroma and detect the chocolate, the black patent—and the grain. Drunk, it has a soft mouth feel, a taste of coffee, a sense of grain, a slight sweetness, and a brief but dry aftertaste. It is excellent.

RECOMMENDED: Mickey Finn's Pale Ale
Mickey Finn's Five Springs Oatmeal Stout

Mishawaka Brewing Co.

3703 N. MAIN ST.

MISHAWAKA, INDIANA 46545

PHONE: 219-256-9994

YEAR ESTABLISHED: 1991

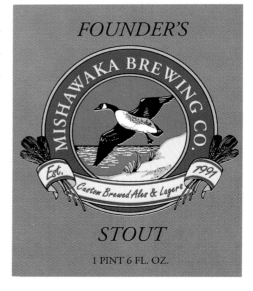

FOUNDER'S

STOUT

1 PINT 6 FL. OZ.

In 1986, Thomas Schmidt, the owner and brewmaster, didn't like beer. He was working for Miles Laboratory, researching the use of enzymes for breweries, and, one fateful day, went to a national microbrewers meeting in Portland, Oregon.

Bingo.

He had the microbrewer's epiphany and, six years later, opened Mishawaka, where he, like so many of his colleagues, makes one exceptional beer and three indifferent ones. Inconsistency is the sign of an immature microbrewery. The irrelevant beers are the equivalent of an adolescent's blemishes, imperfections that hopefully will go away or be smoothed over in time.

Mishawaka Founder's Stout is the treasure, the beer to seek out. Its nose is happily predictable: chocolate and roasty. It goes down full-bodied, rich, and beautifully balanced. And finally, the coda: It has a memory.

The most intriguing aspect of **Lake Effect Pale Ale** is its name. Mishawaka is near Lake Michigan, and depending on the weather, "lake effect" storms develop over the lake, and when the snow comes down, Mr. Schmidt said, "It's fifteen to twenty inches of big, big flakes, a very gentle kind of snow."

The storm may be fulsome, but the ale is underdeveloped. It has the aroma of immature, green hops, and as it is drunk, it is somewhat disparate—very sweet in the middle and very bitter at the end. It isn't a smooth progression.

Mishawaka Amber Ale has a sweet nose, an all-malt flavor and a marked absence of hoppiness. **Mishawaka Four Horsemen Straight Ale** errs on the side of blandness.

RECOMMENDED: Mishawaka Founder's Stout

The Mountain Brewers, Inc.

PO BOX 140

BRIDGEWATER, VERMONT 05034

PHONE: 802-672-5011

FAX: 802-672-5012

YEAR ESTABLISHED: 1989

CAPACITY: 15,000 BARRELS

Mountain Brewers likes to make two kinds of beer: the tried and true, and the wildly experimental. So year-round, they offer the Long Trail Family of Ales, and on whim, the Brown Bag Ales.

Put another way, Brown Bag Ales are the developmental laboratory for Long Trail. To save money and to be free to brew and bottle beers at the spur of a malty-hoppy moment, the Mountain Brewers identifies experimental (maybe it's great, maybe it's not) beers by recycling the Brown Bag Ales label over and over again. No matter what beer is inside the bottle—Ordinary Bitter or Double Bag—the label is the same, except for a stamp that states the style. When a Brown Bag Ale finds a devoted public, it is elevated to the Long Trail Family and anointed with its own label.

The lightest beer is the **Long Trail Kölsch Ale,** which has 15 percent wheat. Open the beer, and there is dismay. There's an off-putting herbal, grassy smell, reminiscent of a barn. But relax. Let the smell blow off and the beer transforms itself into a perfectly palatable ale with a nice malt character and a hoppy shpritz.

The **Long Trail Ale** has a great, tight head, a clean, nice nose, and a wholesome, low-keyed flavor. It is the safe, middle-of-the-road beer, designed to offend no one. It has a soft mouth feel, a balanced flavor where the maltiness is aligned with the hoppiness, and a nice, short aftertaste. It is not aggressive in any way.

But the **Long Trail India Pale Ale** is—in the nose. It opens flowery, hoppy, sweet, and very green. But like the Kölsch, it tastes better than it smells, and the IPA requisite—hoppiness—comes through in the mouth.

Just as the IPA has the proper hoppiness, so, too, does the **Long Trail Brown Ale** possess the necessary sweet flavor. It smells like toast drizzled with cooked maple syrup, with a whiff of chocolate and a little spice. The sweetness is not over-powering, but neither does it have exceptional character.

The joy of microbrewing is to be idiosyncratic, so Andy Pherson, owner and brewmaster, makes **Long Trail Stout,** an Irish-style dry stout without the seductive chocolate nose. "There's no chocolate because we didn't want to," he said. Neither is it heavy.

The stout is toasty, has a little coffee in it, and a nice balance. It ends first with a dry kick, and later, an aftertaste that reverberates.

What, then, lurks in the brown bags?

(A gambler's pleasure, actually. For amusement, you could wager on which of the Brown Bag Ales makes it to the Long Trail Family—and which are tossed out with the spent yeast.)

Ordinary Bitter has promise. It has a light, fresh, balanced nose and a well-hopped flavor. It is closer to an IPA than a classic English bitter. **Double Bag** is for the person who does not like IPAs. Its predominant aroma and flavor is a mild sweetness.

RECOMMENDED: Long Trail Kölsch Ale
Long Trail Ale
Long Trail Pale India Ale
Long Trail Stout
Brown Bag Ordinary Bitter

N ew Glarus Brewing Co.

NEW GLARUS, WISCONSIN 53574

PHONE: 608-527-5850

YEAR ESTABLISHED: 1993

CAPACITY: 6,000 BARRELS

Our little village brewery in New Glarus, Wisconsin is proud to offer to you Edel-Pils. This "Nobel-Pilsner" is the creation of our Brewmaster. He brought a special yeast from Bavaria, combined it with Wisconsin barley and the finest Bavarian and American hops. Then employing traditional brewing methods, this Pilsner is finished with a long cold rest in our cellars. Expect this bier to be creamy and full-bodied with a smooth finish. It will complement any fine meal or friendly gathering. We took our time in brewing so that you might take your time enjoying.

Vielen Dank!

Daniel Carey
Diploma Master Brewer

Edel-Pils

Wisconsin Lager

New Glarus Brewing Co.

12 Fl. Oz.   Brewed and bottled in New Glarus, WI.

We hated the big breweries," said Deborah Carey, whose husband Daniel worked for Anheuser-Busch at Fort Collins, Colorado. "And I was miserable being a corporate wife: 'Do you have a three-car garage? A two-car garage? Where *did* you get your clothes from?'"

In 1993, the Careys moved to New Glarus, he with a Diploma Master Brewer from the Institute of Brewing in London, and she with a business proposal for starting the brewery.

The **Edel-Pils Wisconsin Lager** is a homage to Germany, where Mr. Carey did his apprenticeship. A straightforward lager, it is a pale amber and has a lovely nose, hoppy but with a forward floral scent and a little bit of malt. All the way through from nose to finish, it is a delicious, creamy, full-bodied beer that is full of flavor. Brewed year-round, it is, someone said, a pretty beer. It is also addictive. After one, it is the natural order of things to order a second—and possibly even a third.

"Uff-da is a Norwegian expletive, a joke in Wisconsin," Mrs. Carey said. "Uff-da means 'oh, shit,' as in '*Uff-da,* hot weather.'" Separate the word from the beer, because the **Uff-da Wisconsin Bock Beer** is not a silly beer. It is a strong beer that Mr. Carey said was "brewed to appease the gods of winter."

It will appease anyone who likes a complex beer. It tastes as it looks. Mahogany hued, it has dark, bitter flavors with undertones of chocolate, coffee, and molasses. The second of the two year-round beers, it is made to be served at about 48°F. "The warmer the Bock is, the sweeter it gets," the Careys say.

Made only in the winter, there is **Snowshoe Ale,** an amber Irish ale. It is a spicy, malty beer, with a hint of cinnamon. The hops, however, are evanescent.

Also too sweet and too malty for some palates is **Norski Honey Bock,** brewed for the spring. It's a dessert beer, or what an Australian called a "dolly" beer, a toy beer, not to be drunk with profound, ruminative seriousness.

Moving inevitably toward summer, there is **Solstice Wisconsin Weiss Beer With Yeast**—a Bavarian white beer. (The white refers to the yeast in the unfiltered beer.) It has a malty nose, a creamy head, and a honeyed lemon bite that delights some but is a bit too sweet for others.

Other seasonals include **Coffee Stout, Zwickel Wisconsin Lager With Yeast, Staghorn Octoberfest Beer,** and **Belgian Red Wisconsin Malt Beverage** (brewed with Montmorency cherries).

RECOMMENDED: Edel-Pils Wisconsin Lager
Uff-da Wisconsin Bock Beer
Solstice Wisconsin Weiss Beer With Yeast

North Coast Brewing Co., Inc.

455 NORTH MAIN ST.

FORT BRAGG, CALIFORNIA 95437

PHONE: 707-964-BREW

FAX: 707-964-8768

YEAR ESTABLISHED: 1988

CAPACITY: 15,000 BARRELS

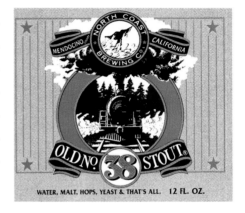

WATER, MALT, HOPS, YEAST & THAT'S ALL.   12 FL. OZ.

I'm older than God," said Tom Allen, fifty-seven, a partner in the brewery, which is owned by three refugees from the advertising world. Mr. Allen markets the beer, Mark Ruedrich brews, and Joe Rosenthal handles finances. The brewery is housed in a 1902 building that has metamorphosed from a mortuary to a church to a junior college to a brewery. Each time, the purpose of the building's occupants has become just a little less serious, or as Mr. Allen said, "one step farther from death."

Ruedrich's Red Seal Ale, a copper red pale ale, opens with a highly spicy nose, and possesses the hoppiness of its style through to the dry finish. To some, it lacks complexity and is a one-note song of hops. But it has its fans, because it accounts for 50 percent of sales.

Blue Star Great American Wheat Beer has a pert, fresh, balanced nose and a light, sweet maltiness. What it does not have is the citric note of a wheat beer, which does it no harm as a delectable, refreshing beer. Still, it tastes more like a golden ale than a true wheat beer.

Old No. 38 Stout has the aroma of the coffee bean, a luscious smokiness, and a voluptuous body. It is a *stout* stout. To be savored.

North Coast also brews **Scrimshaw Pilsner, Alt Nouveau,** and **Oktoberfest Ale.**

RECOMMENDED: Old No. 38 Stout
Blue Star Great American Wheat Beer

Rogue Ales/Oregon Brewing Co.

2320 OSU DR.

NEWPORT, OREGON 97365

PHONE: 503-867-3660

FAX: 503-867-3260

YEAR ESTABLISHED: 1989

A TURN-OF-THE-CENTURY OREGON ROGUE WITH HIS CATCH OF THE DAY. OREGON HISTORICAL SOCIETY #ORHI 86748.

A hint as to what Rogue Ales taste like: The brewmaster is John "More Hops" Maier.

He figures out what to brew, and Jack Joyce, the president and a former lawyer turned marketing expert (Michael Jordan for Nike) turned brewery maven, figures out how to package it.

The packaging is slick ("Here's to the Rogue in you"), the labels (a roguish, mustachioed, bearded fellow) are silk-screened—and the beers are good. Flavor is key.

Ashland Amber Ale has a flowery, roasty, malty nose and a rich, full-bodied, beautifully balanced flavor.

St. Rogue (the rogue holding a halo to his head) **Red Ale** is equally taste. The malty aroma drifts, but doesn't jump, out of the glass. The beer is full bodied, round in the mouth, and finishes with a splendid hoppiness. It is not for those who like their beers pallid.

Maier is a fearless brewer. The **Rogue Scotch Ale** is a *very* alcoholic ale, whose rich, butterscotch intensity is reminiscent of a barley wine. It is the beer to drink instead of eating dessert.

Even more intense is the **Rogue Imperial Stout.** If a stout can be over the top, this is it. It is so high in alcohol, roastiness, bitterness, sweetness, and chocolatyness that it is excessive. A sip is startling; a glassful is overwhelming. As someone said, referring to the Russian heritage of imperial stout (the czars drank it), how cold would it have to have been in Saint Petersburg to make this stout palatable?

Rogue Hazelnut Brown Nectar is, however, flawless. A truly delectable beer, it has a nice roasty, nutty nose and a roundness in the mouth. It tastes malty, yet there are undernotes of hops and a fugitive taste of hazelnuts in the middle. Add hazelnuts to beer. Add them to coffee. It's hard to go wrong.

The brewmaster also makes beers on demand. "We never listen to anyone on the distribution side," Mr. Joyce said. "We listen to consumers and retailers."

So, what is it that drinkers want? And, for that matter, what is it that *women* drinkers want?

Sometimes, the public wants **Rogue Smoke,** a rauchbier. "We make it when we get orders for it," said Mr. Joyce, who admitted it's not to his taste. "To me, you're drinking a barbecue."

Year-round, there is a craving for **Rogue-n-Berry,** a fruit ale with marionberries, which, Mr. Joyce said, is not the brewmaster's favorite beer. But apparently it is the public's, because in 1994, Rogue-n-Berry was the brewery's best-selling beer.

At Rogue's three brewpubs or tasting rooms, it is not necessarily women who are drinking either the fruit ales or the lighter beers. "At our place, it's not so that women drink light," Mr. Joyce said. "I think women talk light and drink dark."

The brewery also offers, in bottles, **Shakespeare Stout, Rogue Ale, Rogue Maierbock, Rogue Golden Ale, Rogue New Porter, Mo Ale,** a wheat beer, **Mexicali Rose** (spiced with smoked jalapeños), and **Mogul Ale.**

RECOMMENDED: Ashland Amber Ale
St. Rogue Red Ale
Rogue Scotch Ale
Rogue Hazelnut Brown Nectar

Otter Creek Brewing, Inc.

74 EXCHANGE ST.

MIDDLEBURY, VERMONT 05753

PHONE: 802-388-0727

YEAR ESTABLISHED: 1991

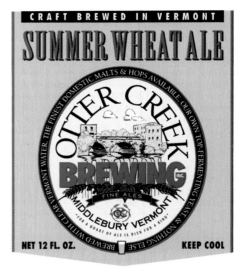

David Ebner, the general manager, tells the story of the origin of Otter Creek, and the gist is this: If you send a child to college in the Pacific Northwest, what he will retain may be a passion for microbrewing and not necessarily for Shakespeare. Or Einstein. Or Wittgenstein.

According to Mr. Ebner, Lawrence Miller, the twenty-nine-year-old owner and brewmaster, went to Reed College in Oregon, started home brewing, chose Middlebury, Vermont, as the place to brew, went to Europe, studied beer (could it be by tasting it?), and opened Otter Creek.

Mr. Miller brews with a very light hand. The **Summer Wheat Ale** has a brief alcoholic moment. It is a light beer, with a slight hint of honey and an equally slight hint of lemon. It is very ephemeral.

So, too, the **Copper Ale.** It isn't as light a beer, and it has an appealing sweetness in the nose and palate, but it's under-hopped. It lacks grip.

Stovepipe Porter has the proper chocolate and roasted notes, but it's abrupt. Flavors don't linger. They disappear, wham-bang.

Mr. Miller also makes **Helles Alt Beer, Hickory Switch Smoked Amber Ale,** and **Mud Bock Spring Ale.**

Of the beers tasted, they are made for those who are faint of palate.

RECOMMENDED (LIGHTLY): Otter Creek Summer Wheat Ale

Otto Brothers' Brewing Co.

PO BOX 4177

JACKSON HOLE, WYOMING 83001

PHONE: 307-733-9000

YEAR ESTABLISHED: 1988

CAPACITY: 850 BARRELS

Hamlet wondered, "To be or not to be." Charlie and Ernie Otto asked: Geology or beer?

Beer won.

The brothers, both trained geologists, have the right brewers' instincts, but the beers lack guts.

Old Faithful Ale, named after the geyser in Yellowstone Park, is an American pale ale. It has a beautiful head but very little flavor.

Drinking **Teton Ale,** an amber ale, is the beer equivalent of darting between the raindrops. The beer has flavor, but it's tucked away between the bubbles. It has a spicy, slightly floral, malty nose, a well-balanced palate leaning toward hoppiness—but it's a little thin and overly carbonated.

The roasty **Moose Juice Stout** is purposefully brewed to be a light stout, or—put another way—a starter stout. It's a stout that could be drunk on a summer day.

RECOMMENDED: Moose Juice Stout

Park Slope Brewing Co., Inc.

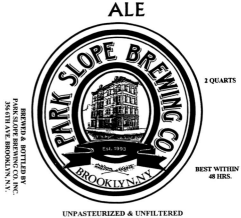

ALE

BREWED & BOTTLED BY
PARK SLOPE BREWING CO. INC.
356 6TH AVE. BROOKLYN, N.Y.

2 QUARTS

Est. 1993

BEST WITHIN
48 HRS.

UNPASTEURIZED & UNFILTERED
KEEP REFRIGERATED

356 SIXTH AVE.

BROOKLYN, NEW YORK 11215

PHONE: 718-788-1756

YEAR ESTABLISHED: 1994

Park Slope does not bottle its beers and so does not belong in this book, were it not for one small thing.

It was at this cozy, irresistibly friendly brewpub that I saw beer made, from nine in the morning until seven at night, one day in February so very long ago. I had my own epiphany. Brewing, I discovered, was a form of cooking, an alcoholic alchemy of fresh greeny hops, crunchy, nutty malts, mysterious yeast that sometimes lives for years, and the most essential liquid—water.

Steven Deptula, who co-owns the brewpub with Eugene Kalenick, his brother-in-law, was the alchemist. And many of the eight rotating house beers are good. They are what they purport to be.

135

Segueing from the lightest to the strongest beers, the **California Pale Ale** has a fresh but unfinished hoppy nose, as if you'd stuck your nose into a fermentation vat.

Best Bitter, on the other hand, is excellent. It starts off with a reticent nose, with some malt, but no floral notes, and a good bitterness in the mouth. It is pleasingly thick in the middle—a sought-after quality in beer.

The **Amber Ale** is for those who like their beer to end on a sweet, not dry note. There's a malty, caramel nose and a good balance, but a cloying finish.

Hopheads will gravitate to the **India Pale Ale,** which has dry, floral notes, a bitterness that develops in the mouth, and a nice dry finish. It aims to please.

The **Porter** was slightly grainy, had the expected hints of bittersweet chocolate, lacked a strong middle, but ended dry and tasty.

The **Irish Dry Stout** was even better. It had the classic nose—espresso with chocolate shavings—smelled sweeter than it tasted, and had a lovely soft, velvety middle and a clean, dry finish.

Park Slope also has its own batch of whimsical beers. On that February Saturday, they were making a pumpkin ale, in the style of Bill ("I don't want lunch! I want BEER!") Owens. They also had on hand **Big Shippy's Barley Wine.** And who was Big Shippy?

Mr. Deptula first apologized. "I'm against silly names," he said, but then he told the story of Big Shippy.

"He was our brewcat, a tomcat, an old cat," Mr. Deptula said of the black-and-white cat who died in December 1994 at the age of eighteen. Big Shippy was not any old feline. He was as gentle with people as he was ferocious with dogs. He was a warrior cat. "He used to attack dogs," Mr. Deptula said. "He even chomped a rottweiler."

So, in this place where one cat once ruled over dogs, the atmosphere is distinctly that of a neighborhood—welcoming and easy. On a Saturday in February, from lunch through to early dinner, patrons included infants and people who were at that age of reckoning: fifty. There were couples on dates and parents with children. Mothers nursed babies while toddlers lurched around the brewpub, clutching onto legs of chairs. Waiters didn't get nervous. Neither did parents.

RECOMMENDED: **Best Bitter**
India Pale Ale
Porter
Irish Dry Stout

Pavichevich Brewing Company

383 ROMANS RD.

ELMHURST, ILLINOIS 60126

PHONE: 630-617-5252

FAX: 630-617-5259

YEAR ESTABLISHED: 1989

CAPACITY: 40,000 BARRELS

Can you taste the lineage of the brewmaster in the beer itself?

With the beers from this brewery, **Baderbräu Pilsener** and **Baderbräu Bock,** the answer is maybe.

Doug Babcock, the vice president and master brewer, was also the master brewer at Stroh Brewing Company in Detroit—a national brewery, not a microbrewery.

What he has brewed, someone said, are safe, commercial beers. The Baderbräu Pilsener has a light nose, a crisp, light body with a touch of malty sweetness, and a clean finish. It is what a pilsener should be.

The Baderbräu Bock is likewise on the light side. Bock is the German name for a strong beer, but this beer is an understated version of its style. It has a discreet nose, a little molasses, and a hint of alcoholic zest.

RECOMMENDED: Baderbräu Pilsener

ete's Brewing Company

514 HIGH ST.

PALO ALTO, CALIFORNIA 94301

PHONE: 415-328-7383

FAX: 415-327-3675

YEAR ESTABLISHED: 1986

In the beer world, Pete Slosberg is a late bloomer. A wine maven, he never drank beer until 1979. His original dream was to make wine in the style of Stag's Leap cabernet sauvignon, but after calculating for fermentation and storage, he learned he would have to wait five to ten years before he could drink it. What, then, was an impatient man to do? He went to Wine and the People, a store in Berkeley, California, and was told he could make white wine that could be drunk in one or two years—or he could make beer.

"I said I didn't like beer," Pete said. Later, he drank his words.

Pete's Wicked Ale is a dark, perfectly balanced brown ale. It is perky and *nice*.

So, too, **Pete's Wicked Red,** an amber ale. It has a sweet, bright flavor with a floral character that someone likened to rosewater.

His seasonals fared less well. **Pete's Wicked Winter Brew** is rife with raspberries, a flavor that horrifies some but entices others. It is a thin beer, which seems seasonally inappropriate. In the winter, beers, like food and clothing, should have substance—even in California.

Pete's Wicked Summer Brew errs on the side of sweetness. It lacks bitterness and leaves on the mouth a residual, nonrefreshing sweetness.

RECOMMENDED: Pete's Wicked Ale
Pete's Wicked Red

The Pike Brewing Co.

1432 WESTERN AVE.

SEATTLE, WASHINGTON 98101

PHONE: 206-622-3373

YEAR ESTABLISHED: 1989

Liberty Malt Supply Company

1419 FIRST AVENUE

SEATTLE, WASHINGTON 98101

PHONE: 206-622-1880

To be in the Pacific Northwest without knowing Charlie Finkel is like being in the San Francisco area without meeting Bill ("I don't want lunch! I want BEER!) Owens.

Charlie Finkel's life *is* beer. He imports it, makes it, drinks it, and writes about it. And just as Belgium can boast a museum devoted solely to the beverage, so, too, can the state of Washington. For in the pristine basement of Mr. Finkel's Liberty Malt Supply Company (an immaculate home brew shop), he has founded the Seattle Microbrewery Museum.

As the founder of Merchant du Vin, Mr. Finkel imports Samuel Smith beers from England and Lindemans beers from Belgium. At his shop, he has coined the slogan: "I came, I saw, I home brewed." So badly does he want people to know the glories of beer that he encourages his customers to reach into the barrels of malts, grab a few kernels, and pop them into the mouth like popcorn. At the rear of the store his staff dispenses tiny plastic cups full of whatever beer is ready that day—brewed, of course, at his Pike Brewing Company just a few blocks away.

Downstairs in the malt shop is the fledgling museum. In the spring of 1995, Mr. Finkel had just begun to display some of the thousands of pieces of beer memorabilia he owns. There were beer signs and beer bottles; beer-related time lines (how many breweries in the United States from the nineteenth century on) and beer-related photographs, including one of Native American women picking hops.

"Hops!" Mr. Finkel said. "They were introduced in the sixteenth century to the English, but before, beer was bittered with herbs! Bog myrtle! Oregano! Rosemary and honey!"

As for his own beers, they are very tasty.

The flagship beer is **Pike Pale Ale,** a quintessential Pacific Northwest beer brewed by and for hopheads. The beer pours with a lush head and has a beautifully balanced palate, with the hops clearly predominating over the malts.

Pike also brews **5X Stout, East India Pale Ale, Birra Preffetto,** flavored with oregano, **Cerveza Russanna,** spiced with chili, **Oyster Stout,** spiked with oyster liquor, and **Old Bawdy Barley Wine.**

The brewery stands on the site of the old LaSalle Hotel, "a house of ill-repute from the 1920s through the 1940s," Mr. Finkel said. Old Bawdy is brewed and named in homage to the brewery's former occupants.

RECOMMENDED: Pike Pale Ale

Portland Brewing Co.

2073 N.W. 31ST ST.

PORTLAND, OREGON 97210

PHONE: 503-226-7623

YEAR ESTABLISHED: 1986

If Portland's four bottled beers have a singular characteristic, it is a sweetness that, while not cloying, is inevitable. These are not beers for the confirmed and devout hophead.

When Mac MacTarnahan, an eighty-year-old man who lives in Beaverton, Oregon, became the largest stockholder at Portland Brewing Co., he inadvertently bought himself immortality by getting a beer named after him. As they say at the brewpub, "Gimme a Mac's, please."

What arrives on the table is **MacTarnahan's Ale,** an amber ale that has a medium body and a well-balanced palate, tilting toward maltiness. "Mac calls himself the Betty Crocker of the microbrewery movement," said Fred Bowman, vice president and one of the cofounders of the company.

Also verging toward sweetness is **Portland Ale,** the first beer

Mr. Bowman designed, in 1988. The nose is malty, and so is the flavor.

Oregon Honey Beer is what an Australian called another "dolly" (meaning "pretty") beer. It is a light summer beer with a neutral sweetness and just a little hint of honey in the aftertaste. "Eighty-eight percent of it is sold in California," Mr. Bowman said. "*Southern* California."

Even lighter in beeriness is **Wheat Berry Brew.** Made with marionberries, the beer instantly provokes jokes about Marion Berry, the mayor-turned-crack addict-turned-mayor of Washington, D.C. The beer has a sweet-sour flavor and scarcely resembles beer as most people know it.

"I'm not a fan of berry beer," Mr. Bowman said as he sipped his own Wheat Berry Brew. "I'm trying to enjoy it myself." A few sips later, he said, "I don't think of it as a beer."

Fruit beers are to beer what wine coolers are to wine—soft drinks with just a tiny zap of alcohol.

RECOMMENDED: MacTarnahan's Ale

Potomac River Brewing Company

14141-A PARKE LONG COURT

CHANTILLY, VIRGINIA 22021

PHONE: 703-631-5430

YEAR ESTABLISHED: 1993

CAPACITY: 3,500 BARRELS

Potomac inspires assorted clichés.

One: Good things come from small breweries.

Two: You *can* teach old dogs new tricks.

Potomac is barely two years old and offers only three beers—at least two of which (the ones tasted) were delectable. Jerry Russell is the fifty-seven-year-old owner and brewmaster who spent twenty-seven years in the navy, retired as a captain, and turned his hobby—home brewing—into his profession.

His **Patowmack Ale** is a properly made beer that pours with a good head and has a fresh hop smell, a malty character, and a full body.

The **Rappahannock Red Ale** is a classic Irish ale—very malty with some hops showing through and ending with a spicy, nutmeg finish.

(The third beer is **Mount Vernon Porter.**)

RECOMMENDED: Patowmack Ale
Rappahannock Red Ale

Redhook Ale Brewery

3400 PHINNEY AVE. NORTH

SEATTLE, WASHINGTON 98103

ALSO WOODINVILLE, WASHINGTON, AND PORTSMOUTH, NEW HAMPSHIRE

PHONE: 206-548-8000

FAX: 206-548-1305

YEAR ESTABLISHED: 1982

CAPACITY: 600,000 BARRELS

Can a microbrewery find happiness allied with Anheuser-Busch?

For Redhook, the answer is yes.

In 1994, Anheuser-Busch paid $18 million for a 25 percent interest in Redhook, a deal out of which A-B gets new products and Redhook gains national distribution. This alliance, beer experts say, is the first in what will certainly become an industry tend.

For Redhook, which makes excellent beers (packaged with bold, slick graphics), the crucial question will be, do the beers stay tasty?

In mid-1995, shortly after the Woodinville Brewery had opened but before the one at Portsmouth had broken ground, the beers were still superb. Never mind that the bottling machines were now handling 450 bottles a minute, or that 10 percent of sales in the Seattle pub was just in souvenir clothes. "Bigness" hadn't yet destroyed what made Redhook successful: fulsome, flavorful beers.

"No one here drinks it," said Pamela Hinckley, vice president and marketing manager, of **Wheat Hook** beer. Of course not. True hopheads, which are what populates the Pacific Northwest, often scoff at wheat beers. Still, Wheat Hook is a nice beer. It has a perfect blend of maltiness and hoppiness and a light, smoky wheat character.

ESB, the extra special bitter ale, is lighter in color than a true ESB, but it is an excellent beer. It has a balanced nose, what Ms. Hinckley calls a "perfect middle," and an appealing maltiness that is not cloyingly sweet.

Ballard Bitter India Pale Ale does what it's supposed to do. Its intense hoppiness and dry, crisp finish both refreshes you and makes you want more.

Blackhook Porter is closer to a stout than a porter. It has a stout's deep, dark roasted coffee aroma, a dry, hoppy taste, and a long, bitter aftertaste.

Redhook also makes a **Winterhook Christmas Ale** available only in the winter, and another series of experimental and occasional beers under its Blueline label.

RECOMMENDED: Wheat Hook
Redhook ESB
Ballard Bitter India Pale Ale
Blackhook Porter

Rio Bravo Restaurant & Brewery

515 CENTRAL AVE. N.W.

ALBUQUERQUE, NEW MEXICO 87102

PHONE: 505-242-6800

YEAR ESTABLISHED: 1993

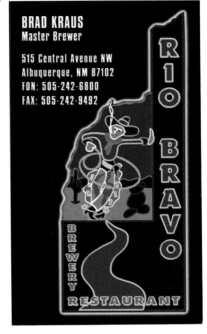

BRAD KRAUS
Master Brewer

515 Central Avenue NW
Albuquerque, NM 87102
FON: 505-242-6800
FAX: 505-242-9492

Rio Bravo is proof that you should never judge a beer by its label. The black ink runs on the white label, and the graphic design consists of the name, address, and ingredients. There are no pictures, logos, or colors. The packaging is the beer equivalent to generic food products in a supermarket—plain and serviceable. But since it's what's inside that counts, Rio Bravo is a microbrewery to watch.

It makes only three beers, and each is excellent.

Coronado Gold is a blond ale with a light nose, an addictively hoppy flavor with a toasty maltiness, and a clean, crisp hop finish. It is the perfect ale for a lager drinker.

High Desert Pale Ale is the flagship beer, the best-seller. Amber in color, it has a spicy but not overwhelming nose and a caramel maltiness balanced by a firm hoppiness (Chinook and Cascade).

Brad Kraus, the brewmaster and a partner, calls the **Esteban Dark** a porter, and it is true to style. It has a lovely roasty nose and all the expected and nevertheless delectable hints of chocolate, coffee, and licorice. Lisa Smith, another partner, calls it "a lusty, malty dark ale in the porter style." That, too.

RECOMMENDED: Coronado Gold
High Desert Pale Ale
Esteban Dark

Riverside Brewing Co.

1229 COLUMBIA AVE., SUITE C4

RIVERSIDE, CALIFORNIA 92507

PHONE: 909-682-5465

FAX: 909-682-5487

YEAR ESTABLISHED: 1993

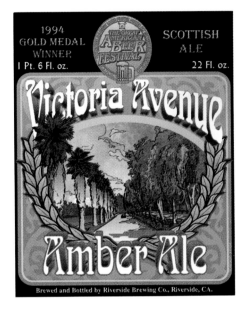

Barely two years old, Riverside is an emerging microbrewery whose beers are slightly uneven.

The **Victoria Avenue Amber Ale** is a nicely balanced, thick, full-bodied ale with a good malty character and a mild sweetness that lingers in the aftertaste.

The **7th Street Stout** is a light-bodied stout with a roasty, sweet toffee nose. The lightness makes it highly quaffable, but also less memorable. The stout, although tasty, is cut-and-dried, somewhat abrupt. It lacks one of stout's greatest characteristics—a tendency to linger. And linger. Even when the flavor of a stout has disappeared from the tongue, it should hover in the mind.

Pullman Pale Ale has a nicely balanced nose and a neutral malty character, with a lot of hops coming through. It is a presentable beer.

For those who like a beer whose head is so creamy it looks like a great fluff of meringue, there is **Raincross Cream Ale.** The three-inch head is its most notable trait. The flavor is lemony, the body thin.

RECOMMENDED: Victoria Avenue Amber Ale
7th Street Stout

Rockies Brewing Company

2880 WILDERNESS PLACE

BOULDER, COLORADO 80301

PHONE: 303-444-8448

FAX: 303-444-4796

YEAR ESTABLISHED: 1979

CAPACITY: 42,000 BARRELS

Owning a microbrewery may be fun—instant gratification, glorious flavors, millions of dollars pouring in—but no one ever said it was easy.

Rockies Brewing Company is an incarnation of what was originally the Boulder Brewing Company, which was founded in 1979. In 1983, the company went public. The next year, it built a new microbrewery. By 1990, it was in foreclosure.

That summer, Gina Day and Diane Greenlee took over the lease, David Zuckerman became the brewmaster, and Boulder Beer Company was born. By 1993, the name had changed again. The brewery was no longer micro. It wanted to be regional, and so the new name—Rockies Brewing Company—signified the intent.

The company makes six ales year-round: **Boulder Extra Pale Ale, Boulder Porter, Buffalo Gold Premium Ale, Boulder Amber Ale, Boulder Stout,** and **Rockies Premium Ale.**

Only the last was tasted—and it is a flawless lawn-mowing beer. It is nicely balanced, light-bodied, with a touch of sweetness in the finish.

Seasonally, the brewery makes **Boulder Cliffhanger Ale, Boulder Fall Festival, Boulder Extra Special Bitter, Boulder Igloo Ale,** and **Boulder Single Track.**

RECOMMENDED: Rockies Premium Ale

Saint Arnold Brewing Company

2522 FAIRWAY PARK DR.

HOUSTON, TEXAS 77092

PHONE: 713-686-9494

FAX: 713-686-9474

YEAR ESTABLISHED: 1994

CAPACITY: 4,500 BARRELS

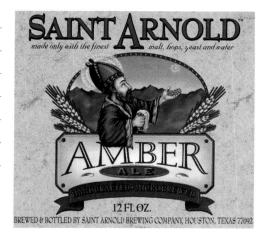

From a man's sweat and God's love, beer came into the world," said Saint Arnold, the bishop (580 to 640) of Metz, France, and the patron saint of brewers. During the plague years, when water became unsafe for consumption, Saint Arnold urged the peasants to drink beer—and the peasants reverently obeyed. Not only was Saint Arnold popular, but he also brought about a miracle: the mug of beer that never ran dry.

In 640, Saint Arnold died at a monastery near Remiremont, and the next year the citizens of Metz asked that his body be exhumed and ceremoniously carried to their city for reburial in the Church of the Holy Apostles. When the procession reached the town of Champigneulles, the porters stopped to rest, and, of course, to have a beer.

Voilà! A miracle.

In the whole town, there was only one mug of beer for the thirsty pilgrims. But all that day, as the pilgrims drank and drank, the mug never ran dry.

Brock Wagner, the brewmaster who owns the brewery with Kevin Bartol, wouldn't mind providing an endless stream of beer for the people of Texas, even if the local water is now perfectly safe to drink.

The two owners (Mr. Wagner is thirty, Mr. Bartol, thirty-five) are former investment bankers who loved their former work but not their colleagues. "It's an industry driven by money," Mr. Wagner said, "and it's a wonderful career if money is your sole goal in life."

Making beer (and money) are the partners' goals.

Year-round, they brew three beers. **Saint Arnold Kristall Weizen** has a fresh, slightly green-hopped, floral nose, a sweet-lemony fruitiness, and a minimal aftertaste.

Saint Arnold Amber Ale is a nicely balanced, strong hoppy beer.

The third beer, **Saint Arnold Brown Ale,** starts off strong, with a malty, blackstrap molasses character, which is then undercut by a sharp, bittersweet chocolate flavor that errs on the side of harshness.

RECOMMENDED: Saint Arnold Amber Ale

San Francisco Brewing Company

155 COLUMBUS AVE.

SAN FRANCISCO, CALIFORNIA
94133

PHONE: 415-434-3344

YEAR ESTABLISHED: 1985

CAPACITY: 1,000 BARRELS

SAN FRANCISCO BREWING COMPANY.

FROM GRAIN TO GLASS

The 1906 San Francisco fire and earthquake leveled the city, and the three-thousand-mile trip from San Francisco to Manhattan leveled one of the brewery's four hand-bottled, unpasteurized, and unfiltered beers. But what survived to be tasted had promise.

The **Emperor Norton Lager** was the delectable, cohesive beer. It has a pleasant malt character in the palate, a proper balance, a full body, and a sweet richness.

Two beers hinted of goodness that presumably increases with one's proximity to the source—namely, the tap. The **Andromeda Hefe Weizen** had a spicy nose, a hint of sweet clove, and enough flavor to render it not quite innocuous. The **Shanghai PA** (pale ale) starts off ignominiously with a green-hopped nose but improves in the mouth. The palate reveals itself to be nicely hoppy and balanced. Brisk, however, it's not.

The **Pony Express Ale** smells like orange pekoe tea and arrived very thin of body, with just a touch of hops.

There are also **Albatross Lager, Gripman's Porter, Alcatraz Stout,** and **Oofty Goofty Barley Wine.**

The brewery has a history behind it. Built in 1907 as the Andromeda Saloon, it is the last of the Barbary Coast saloons still standing.

And if location is everything, then the brewery is brilliantly situated. On the corner of Columbus and Pacific Avenues, it is smack-dab at the intersection of Chinatown, North Beach, and the financial district. For San Francisco, a languid city, this is an area with a detectable rhythm.

Chinese vendors sell their roasted ducks. Deadheads prowl the streets, their ponytails graying, tie-dyed shirts fading. Last year, on Christmas Eve day, the local bars and coffeehouses were half full and convivial. People sat, some animated, others daydreaming, but not one looking lonely as they sipped espresso, wine, or, of course, beer.

RECOMMENDED: Emperor Norton Lager
Andromeda Hefe Weizen

Schirf Brewing Company/ Wasatch Brew Pub

PO BOX 459

PARK CITY, UTAH 84060

PHONE: 801-645-9500

YEAR ESTABLISHED: 1986

CAPACITY: 8,600 BARRELS

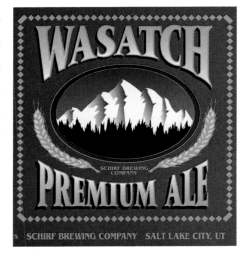

Schirf Brewing Company is very nearly an oxymoron. It's in a state where about 50 percent of the population—the Mormons—don't drink.

"I found the toughest test market I could find," said Gregory Schirf, the president and founder. "When 50 percent of the market doesn't consume our product, it's incumbent for *us* to drink it."

The flagship beer, **Wasatch Premium Ale,** is the brewery's first—and best—beer. Amber in color, it doesn't have much of a nose, but it does possess a creamy head and a healthy balance of malts and hops.

Wasatch Slickrock Lager is named after red sandstone formations in southern Utah, and the name is more interesting than the beer. Bitterness registers in what is otherwise a vague, nebulous taste reminiscent of nonalcoholic beers.

The **Wasatch Raspberry Wheat Beer** suffers from the same ills common to many American fruit beers. The raspberry smell is overpowering and speaks of cough syrups and lozenges rather than beer. The flavor leans toward fruity and sour. Mr. Schirf said the raspberry notes were subtle, but subtlety (like truth) is relative.

From two breweries, one in Salt Lake City, the other in Park City, Schirf also offers an **Apricot Hefeweizen,** an **Irish Stout,** and other seasonal beers.

In 2002, Utah will host the Winter Olympics. Surely, those athletes (and the spectators) will be thirsty for beer. Not everyone is a Mormon.

RECOMMENDED: **Wasatch Premium Ale**

Sierra Nevada Brewing Co.

1075 EAST 20TH ST.

CHICO, CALIFORNIA 95928

PHONE: 916-893-3520

YEAR ESTABLISHED: 1981

CAPACITY: 200,000 BARRELS

Ask a microbrewery aficionado (the kind who likes his beers hoppy) what his favorite beers are, and as inevitably as night follows day, as beer makes people burp, out will come the words "Sierra Nevada."

Sierra Nevada is a household word for two reasons: longevity and excellence. But in 1978, when Ken Grossman and Paul Camusi started building the brewery, they hadn't a clue that they were helping to start a *trend*. What they did know was that they both loved to home brew, that Anchor was producing superb beers, and that in Sonoma, New Albion was the first microbrewery in the United States since Prohibition.

"We made a trip to New Albion, saw they were brewing forty-five gallons a batch, which is five hundred barrels a year, looked at their equipment and thought, geeze, we could do that," Mr. Grossman said.

For $5,250 they bought a used soda-pop bottling line (since discarded), and by 1981 were in business.

Astonishingly, the recipes, which are Mr. Grossman's, have not changed. The **Sierra Nevada Pale Ale** is the flagship beer, the one that made Chico famous. Eighty percent of the company's sales are the Pale Ale. It is a flawless beer that opens with bright, perky high notes of maltiness and orange blossom and segues into a delectable hoppiness.

The **Sierra Nevada Porter** has hints of chocolate, cinnamon, and licorice, and is an appropriately dry, medium-bodied ale.

A roastiness prevails in the rich, dark, full-bodied **Sierra Nevada Stout.**

On a seasonal rotation, there are **Bigfoot Barleywine Style Ale, Pale Bock** (a lager), **Summerfest** (also a lager), and **Celebration Ale.**

There will never be a fruit beer. "I'm a traditionalist," said Mr. Grossman, the brewmaster. "Fruit beers bridge the gap between the soda pop and beer generation and are for people who like a sweet, syrupy, nondescript beer flavor with cherry or blueberry overtones."

Yecch.

An elder of the microbrewery movement, Mr. Grossman analyzes the differences between starting with a microbrewery or a brewpub. Since 1978, the market has changed. "In 1978, we had to be in bottles," he said. "Draft beer was not as well received as it is now. Now, our business is one-third draft and two-third bottles. Draft beer is technically easier to do. But if you want to have beer available in a lot of outlets, bottles are the way to go. But the two are symbiotic. They each sell the other."

He advises the fledgling brewer to figure out the market and the goal. "If you're going to market the beer in a small, regional area, and can get a few hundred accounts—and your goals *aren't* to be all over the United States—you can go draft only. But most brewers who go into draft only eventually go into bottling."

The reason why people suddenly spend anywhere from

$1 million to $2 million for a new bottling line that can do two hundred to four hundred bottles a minute is purely ambition. Even at 200,000 barrels a year, Sierra Nevada is thinking expansion. It may open a second brewery on its property and double its capacity, Mr. Grossman said. Asked whether they want to be bought by a Big Three brewery, as Redhook was by Anheuser-Busch, he said no. "We want to keep it local," he said. He wants to brew his own beers—none of them fruit.

RECOMMENDED: Sierra Nevada Pale Ale
Sierra Nevada Porter
Sierra Nevada Stout

Snake River Brewing Co., Inc./Jackson Hole Pub and Brewery

PO BOX 3319

JACKSON HOLE, WYOMING 83001

PHONE: 307-739-2337

YEAR ESTABLISHED: 1994

CAPACITY: 4,000 BARRELS

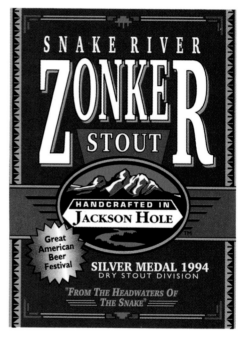

Albert Upsher, the owner, has had three careers in fifty-five years. He was a securities analyst on Wall Street, became a beer wholesaler for Anheuser-Busch, and in 1994 started Snake River. "Am I supposed to change occupations every ten years?" he asked. "I don't know. But I did."

As with many new microbreweries, two of the year-round beers are good, and one needs work.

Snake River Lager is a well-made, well-balanced beer with a slight malt character, a full, creamy mouth, and a clean finish and aftertaste. It is highly likable.

In the quiet world of fly-fishing, a *zonker* is a white-and-black fishing fly. It is also the name given to the brewery's stout, the touted signature beer.

Zonker Stout is not necessarily Mr. Upsher's favorite beer. "I've never been much of a stout drinker," he said. But Zonker Stout is the beer of the moment because it is the first Snake River beer to win a silver medal (or any kind of medal, for that matter) at the 1994 Great American Beer Festival in Denver, just eight months after the brewery opened.

It deserves its praise. It has a roasty, toasty, nutty aroma, a rich, full body, and the surprise of more hops in the mouth than in the nose.

The beer that is still having growing pangs is the **Snake River Pale Ale.** There's a green hoppy character in the nose, as if you'd put your nose in a bag of raw hops, and when the beer is poured, the glass fills not just with ale but with the fumes of carbon dioxide.

Seasonally, Snake River brews a **Bald Eagle Bock, Custer's Last Ale,** an **India Pale Ale,** an **Alpine Fest Bier,** and an **Oat Meal Porter.**

RECOMMENDED: Snake River Zonker Stout
Snake River Lager

Stoudt Brewing Co.

PO BOX 880, ROUTE 272

ADAMSTOWN, PENNSYLVANIA
  19501

PHONE: 717-484-4387

YEAR ESTABLISHED: 1987

CAPACITY: 4,500 BARRELS

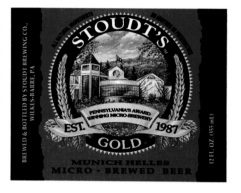

In 1987, in the verdant countryside sixty miles west of Philadelphia, Carol Stoudt, one of the industry's few women brewers, started making beer. "For the first few years, I wasn't taken seriously," Mrs. Stoudt said. Even in 1995, she was still learning—switching from green glass to brown to better protect the beer in the twenty-two-ounce bottles. She was also having problems with her distributors.

She brews both lagers and ales, and many of the beers are excellent. Among the lagers, the **Stoudt's Gold** has an enticing floral nose, a medium maltiness, and a pert, clean, hoppy finish.

The **Stoudt's Mai-Bock** smells sweeter than it tastes. It starts off with a sweet malt character in the nose but moves quickly into a nice, smooth, malty-hoppy palate. It is a delicious, full-bodied lager.

So, too, the **Bock Reserve Beer,** which tastes like a doppel-bock. It is a strong, thick, heavy beer, with a slight molasses in the nose and a not-to-be-scoffed-at alcoholic afterglow. The **Stoudt's Fest** pales in comparison to the other beers. It has a sweet malt nose and is properly balanced, but lacks a strong personality.

The **Abbey Double,** an unfiltered Belgian abbey–style ale, had a sweet pink bubblegum quality underlined by alcohol. Not a success.

Neither was the **Stout.** Possibly a bad bottle that hadn't been stored properly, it was empty and acrid and lacked all the glorious characteristics—roastiness, chocolate, coffee, full-bodied bliss—of its style.

Stoudt also makes a **Pilsener,** a **Honey Double Bock,** and an **Abbey Triple.**

RECOMMENDED: Stoudt's Gold
Stoudt's Mai-Bock
Stoudt's Bock Reserve Beer
Stoudt's Fest

Sudwerk Privatbrauerei Hübsch

1107 KENNEDY PLACE, NO. 1

DAVIS, CALIFORNIA 95616

PHONE: 916-756-2739

YEAR ESTABLISHED: 1990

CAPACITY: 8,000 BARRELS

Dave Sipes, the brewmaster, is batting .500. Two of the beers are tasty, and two are not.

Start with the **Hübsch Märzen,** a very malty, seasonal, springtime beer. It has a red-amber color and a properly balanced palate.

For those who like a crisp beer, there is **Hübsch Lager,** which is a straight-ahead, light-bodied beer with a neutral, balanced palate. It is not remarkable. Neither does it offend.

The **Hübsch Hefe Weizen Wheat Beer** smelled strangely like salami and had a harsh, bitter edge. The **Hübsch Pilsner** was also in dire trouble, with a funky nose and a bitter taste. The malts had disappeared.

RECOMMENDED: Sudwerk Hübsch Märzen
             Sudwerk Hübsch Lager

Summit Brewing Co.

2264 UNIVERSITY AVE.

SAINT PAUL, MINNESOTA 55114

PHONE: 612-645-5029

YEAR ESTABLISHED: 1986

CAPACITY: 27,000 BARRELS

Taste buds in Saint Paul are not wildly experimental, but that doesn't faze Mark Stutrud, president and head brewer of Summit Brewing Co. "We started out being quite aggressive," he said, "and we've maintained that position."

What is aggressive (full-flavored with the clear presence of the hops) in the Midwest is restrained in the East Coast. But restraint doesn't prohibit tastiness.

The **Summit Extra Pale Ale** has a malty nose with a slight hint of hops, and a happy balance of hops and malts in the palate. The nose is reserved, and there is no aftertaste. But it is a well-made beer.

Summit Great Northern Porter also has the signature understated nose, with rising aromas of cocoa and roasted barley. It is a classic porter, highly quaffable and very appealing.

Not so the **Summit Hefe Weizen.** It arrived in a state of sorry berry decay.

RECOMMENDED: Summit Extra Pale Ale
Summit Great Northern Porter

Wild River Brewing

144 KENROSE LANE

CAVE JUNCTION, OREGON 97523

PHONE: 503-592-3556

595 NORTHEAST E STREET

GRANTS PASS, OREGON 97526

PHONE: 503-471-7487

YEAR ESTABLISHED: 1990

CAPACITY: 2,800 BARRELS

"Blessing of your heart, you brew good Ale."
Shakespeare • Two Gentlemen of Verona

I'm older than the hills," said Hubert Smith, the fifty-six-year-old anthropological filmmaker-turned-brewmaster. "I got tired of importing cameras and exporting films, so I made a lifestyle move to southern Oregon from Los Angeles." There Mr. Smith met Jerry and Bertha Miller, "the guys down the road," who had recently opened Wild River Brewing. Mr. Smith mentioned he used to write about beer, and forthwith—a new job and five excellent year-round beers. (Mr. Smith is also proof that brewing, unlike modeling or playing tennis, is an age-blind profession.)

Wild River may be small. It may even be somewhat unknown. But take note. It is a brewery to be reckoned with. Its beers are consistent and pristine. Even the colors have a certain appealing clarity.

Begin with the **Hefe-Weizen,** a category of beer unto itself. It opens with a delightful fresh aroma that is equal parts wheat and overripe lemon. There is a slightly gamy aroma that is alluring in its exoticism, and a palate that is as well balanced as it is refreshing. It is a Hefe-Weizen with a bit of soul.

Gold is the color of the **Wild River Kölsch,** a nicely balanced, hoppy beer, while the **Wild River Extra Special Bitter** pours a glinting copper. The ESB has a clean, specific, malty nose, an underlying hop character, and a medium body.

Sniff the **Wild River Nut Brown Ale** and discover a winsome, nutty, chocolaty nose. (In a flight of complimentary fancy, someone said it also smelled like the bark of a tree—a very pleasant-smelling tree.) It is slightly sweet, and finishes with a note of burnt caramel.

There are stouts dry (Irish) and stouts sweet (English)—and there are imperial stouts, the strongest of them all. Beware, then, of the **Wild River Double Eagle Imperial Stout.** Wild River cannot be accused of mislabeling. The stout is a beer to be sipped slowly (never gulped), and drunk on its own—without the accompaniment of food.

It is a luscious, voluptuous stout that pours treacly, has a lovely roasted perfume, and a spicy, winey, complex palate. It has warmth and memory, and the alcohol is palpable. It is a stout to make a winter night joyous.

Seasonally, Mr. Smith makes a **Mai Bock, Blackberry Porter, Oktoberfest, Snug Harbor Old Ale,** a strong ale, and **Cave Bear Barley Wine.**

RECOMMENDED: Wild River Hefe-Weizen
Wild River Kölsch
Wild River Nut Brown Ale
Wild River Extra Special Bitter
Wild River Double Eagle Imperial Stout

Willamette Valley Brewing Company

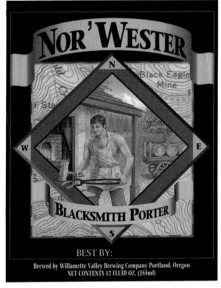

66 S.E. MORRISON ST.

PORTLAND, OREGON 97214

PHONE: 503-232-9771

YEAR ESTABLISHED: 1993

CAPACITY: 40,000 BARRELS

You wouldn't *want* me to brew it," said Jim Bernau, founder of Willamette Valley Brewing Company, whose beer is labeled Nor'Wester. Mr. Bernau grows grapes at his Willamette Valley Vineyards and makes what he says is good wine, but he disclaims any ability to either grow hops or make beer.

Instead, he hires brewers and makes them partners.

Nor'Wester Hefe Weizen is a ghost of a beer, so very light that it is barely there. The wheat aroma is absent; the floral and malt notes are faint, as is the slightly sweet taste.

Nor'Wester Dunkel Weizen is a somewhat more personable beer. It smells more of the malt, but again goes light on the hops and the floral notes.

Hold the **Nor'Wester Blacksmith Porter** up to the light and what do you see? "A Coke, a nice carbonated fizzy Coke," someone said. The bubbles are rampant, the nose nonexistent, but the flavor is quite pleasant—nice and roasty.

As for **Nor'Wester Best Bitter Ale,** you can only mourn. It traveled three thousand miles and turned sour en route.

RECOMMENDED: **Nor'Wester Blacksmith Porter**

Yakima Brewing & Malting Co., Inc./Grant's Pub Brewery

1803 PRESSON PLACE

YAKIMA, WASHINGTON 98902

PHONE: 509-575-1900

YEAR ESTABLISHED: 1981

CAPACITY: 15,000 BARRELS

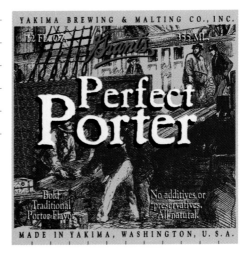

For Bert Grant, who is sixty-seven, life *is* beer. Since the mid-1940s, he has worked only in the world of beer. He was research director with Stroh, technical director with S. S. Steiner, a major hops producer, and, since 1982, has been the owner of Yakima Brewing & Malting Co., whose bottles have labels that read "Grant's."

"I couldn't stand the beer any of the big breweries were making," he said. Up until the early '50s, a lot of ales from Carling's, Molson's, and Labatt's were good, he said. "By 1960, they started watering them down," Mr. Grant said. "By the '70s, they were *all* watery, and by the late '70s, North America lacked any decent beers."

Grant's Celtic Ale is a light beer, a hundred calories per twelve-ounce bottle, and it has the inherent problem of a light beer. It is a lovely dark tea color with reddish tints, but the flavor is bland.

Grant's Weiss Beer has a fresh, clean taste. It is a summer quaffing beer.

Grant's India Pale Ale has a light, cereal nose, tastes more of the malt than of the hops, but has a nice medium hoppiness. The finish, however, is short.

The less light the beer, however, the more splendid it becomes.

Grant's Perfect Porter is, in fact, perfect. It has a wonderful roasty, chocolate, winey smell, with a touch of mint. "It has real breeding," someone said. It finishes dry, yet with a taste of chocolate.

Not only is the porter flawless, but so also is **Grant's Imperial Stout.** It pours treacly, smells roasty, and tastes delicious. It is a full-bodied, rich, robust, high-in-alcohol beer.

He also makes **Grant's Scottish Ale,** which accounts for 50 percent of sales, **Grant's Apple Honey Ale,** and **Grant's Spiced Ale.**

RECOMMENDED: Grant's Weiss Beer
Grant's India Pale Ale
Grant's Perfect Porter
Grant's Imperial Stout

BIBLIOGRAPHY

Briggs, Hough, Stevens, and Young. *Malting and Brewing Science,* Vols. I & II. London: Chapman and Hall, 1981.

Harold Grossman and Harriet Lembeck. *Grossman's Guide to Wines, Beers and Spirit.* New York: Scribner, 1983.

H. S. Rich & Co. *One Hundred Years of Brewing.* Chicago and New York, 1903, reprinted by Arno Press, New York, 1974.

The Institute for Brewing Studies North American Brewers Resource Directory. Boulder, CO: Brewers Publications, 1994–1995.

Michael Jackson's Beer Companion. Philadelphia: Running Press, 1993.

Michael Jackson. *The New World Guide to Beer.* Philadelphia: Running Press, 1988.

Michael Jackson. *The Simon & Schuster Pocket Guide to Beer,* 1994.

Charlie Papazian. *The New Complete Joy of Home Brewing.* New York: Avon Books, 1991.

The Practical Brewer. Madison, WI: Master Brewers Association of the Americas, 1978.

ACKNOWLEDGMENTS

When I started this book, I thought that one could simply gather a group of people together, drink, take notes, and write.

But beer has its own complexities, and *Premier Beer* could not have been written without help from friends.

So, thanks to Ruth Reichl, who suggested that I might need to hire a beer consultant; to Greg Louie, who found me that perfect consultant in Cliff Batuello; and a very special thanks to Cliff, who educated us with each and every sip.

Sue Carswell, my editor at Pocket Books, gave me swift guidance, and Craig Hillman provided tremendous assistance. My editors at the *New York Times*, Barbara Graustark of the Home Section and Trish Hall of the Living Section, offered their encouragement. So, too, did Pam Bernstein, my agent, and Dale Burg and Kathy Casey, two friends.

Three brewers were especially helpful—Stephen Hindy, Bill Owens, and Charlie Finkel.

And, finally, thanks to my daughter Anna, for so graciously explaining to her guests that her mother was not an alcoholic, but that there were four hundred bottles of beer in the house because I was writing this guide.

INDEX